2x 7/10-8/11

French Women
Don't Sleep Alone

French Women Don't Sleep Alone

PLEASURABLE SECRETS TO FINDING LOVE

JAMIE CAT CALLAN

CITADEL PRESS
Kensington Publishing Corp.
www.kensingtonbooks.com

CITADEL PRESS BOOKS are published by

Kensington Publishing Corp.
850 Third Avenue
New York, NY 10022

All Kensington titles, imprints, and distributed lines are available at special
quantity discounts for bulk purchases for sales promotions, premiums,
fund-raising, educational, or institutional use. Special book excerpts or
customized printings can also be created to fit specific needs. For details,
write or phone the office of the Kensington special sales manager:
Kensington Publishing Corp., 850 Third Avenue, New York, NY 10022,
attn: Special Sales Department; phone 1-800-221-2647.

First printing: March 2009

10 9 8 7 6 5 4 3 2 1

Printed in the United States of America

Library of Congress Control Number: 2008936728

ISBN-13: 978-0-8065-3069-7
ISBN-10: 0-8065-3069-3

To Thompson

with love

Le mystère de la femme française
c'est que son homme
sait qu'il peut la perdre à tout moment.

(The mystery of the French woman is that her man
knows he can lose her at any moment.)

Contents

Introduction   1

1   French Women Don't Date   13

2   The Joy of Cooking   32

3   Meeting Men . . . *C'est Facile!*   58

4   French Women "Seduce" Everyone They Meet   73

5   A French Woman Feels Good in Her
    Own Skin   85

6   Beauty and Brains   105

7   French Women Take Care of Their Bodies   117

8   The French Connection: Lingerie   125

9   The Power of the Coterie   140

10 French Women *et le Jardin Secret*   154

11 How French Women Earn Their Reputation
    for Being So Sexy   166

12 *Mariage à la Mode*   176

13 How to Be a French Woman While Living
    in America   187

Acknowledgments   193

French Women
Don't Sleep Alone

♥♥

INTRODUCTION

MY GRANDMOTHER was French.

In all the years of my growing up, I never felt as if I truly understood her. In fact, for a long time, I believed she didn't even really like me. I thought she was rather cold. She was certainly a little aloof. I did love her, passionately. And I admired her too, but there were many times when I envied my friends with their stereotypical gray-haired grandmas— affectionate nannas who wore flowered cotton housedresses and baked sugar cookies and squeezed your cheeks and kissed and hugged you against their soft flesh until you squealed and squirmed away.

My French grandmother did none of these things. She was tall and slim and elegant. Every other Sunday, she arrived at our house in Stamford, Connecticut, in my grandfather's freshly washed and impossibly shiny black Buick. My grandfather always drove because my grandmother never learned to drive. Even so, she never seemed to be without someone to chauffeur her around town.

I was thrilled by the prospect of my grandmother's visits. I knew she would want to observe me, ask me about my dance lessons, tell me to stand up straight and scrutinize my clothes. I always got dressed up for her. I would run to the car and open the passenger-side door to greet her and before she could even stand up, I would ask her if she had any candy for me. This was something I had learned to do from my best friend and her grandmother.

However, my grandmother never had candy. She would snap open her small leather purse and offer me instead a black licorice cough drop. I accepted this as if it was the most delicious and delightful confection in the world and I would thank her. Then my grandmother would lift her stockinged legs out of the car, and emerge to kiss me on each cheek.

Her hair was dark, before she switched over to a silvery rinse. She had long, slender, shapely legs. And she always wore a colorful scarf around her neck. She wore sheer stockings and heels. Her hair was always perfectly coiffed—after all, she spent every Saturday afternoon of her life in the beauty salon. Oh, and she wore a little makeup and always lipstick. She liked the color peach. Not pink. She was very particular. It had to be peach. Her shoes matched her handbag, although they were never a completely matched set. She didn't do anything as obvious as that. She always carried a silk handkerchief with her. She didn't smile a whole lot. She didn't laugh with abandon. She seldom hugged me.

However, she did have perfect posture.

When she arrived, she created a little stir in our suburban neighborhood. She spoke with a slight accent, pronouncing "onion" as "ungion." She was a wonderful cook and taught me to make *tarte tatin*. (And now, I wish I had written down her recipe!)

At my grandparents' home in Devon, Connecticut, they had a garden where they grew turnips, beets, green beans, summer squash, corn, zucchini, and tomatoes—which they jarred for the winter. They also had a peach tree, from which my grandmother made peach jam and peach pie. When we ate at their home, everything was incredibly fresh and completely delicious.

I DIDN'T REALIZE it at the time, but I was growing up under the gentle tutelage of my mysterious French grandmother and I was a witness to the secrets French women have been using for centuries to keep their men intrigued and in a state of constant fascination. It's true that my grandmother and grandfather did not always have the most peaceful relationship. They would occasionally get into fiery spats. When I first witnessed these squabbles I would become very upset. I watched as my grandfather yelled, and my grandmother seethed and put her energies into kneading pie dough, pressing and turning, pounding and rolling out, so that she could make her wonderful apple tart. The disagreement might go on for hours or days, but it would always end the same way—a night of whispers with the bedroom door locked. The next morning my grandmother would return from the department store with a new hat. It didn't take long for me to realize that these quarrels were not simply about disagreeing, but that rather an intricate and sensual dance was taking place. I saw that for a French woman it is more important to hold her ground and to be herself than to always get along and keep the peace, and that sometimes making a delicious pastry is better than open communication, and that not always being the "good girl" can turn up the heat in the bedroom.

WHEN SHE WAS YOUNGER, my grandmother was a singer, a dancer, and a musician, and she even sewed theatrical costumes. The French side of my family is filled with painters and musicians, dancers and singers, and even a puppet-maker. During the 1920s, my grandfather managed a family theatrical troupe that played in theaters across New England. My grandmother sang and played the violin; my mother, with her Shirley Temple ringlets, danced and recited poetry (once on *The Children's Radio Hour* in New York City); and my uncle played the drums. This was during the Great Depression—during the waning years of vaudeville.

I grew up hearing these stories and I wanted to have Shirley Temple ringlets too. When I was little, my grandmother would curl my hair, using strips of cloth made from old linens. I sat patiently as her fingers worked through my freshly washed hair, so that I could go to school on Monday morning with "rag curls," as she called them. I looked at her reflection in the mirror, sitting behind me—her lips pursed, her lovely face deep in concentration—and I thought, I want to be like her, knowing this was ultimately impossible. I was really not like her at all. And she would remain a foreign country to me, a mystery.

By the end of my sixth grade year, all the children were asked to decide what foreign language we would like to study the following year in junior high school. Of course, I wanted to learn French. I'd already tried out my fake French with my friend Joanne. We would go into the A&P and walk down the aisles, pretending we were not American at all and we were "very confused" by the American products— *how you say—Kellogg's Cornflakes?* We laughed a lot, and cried out *oh là là! Mon Dieu!* This was delicious fun, but of course we didn't fool anyone and the storeowner told us that if we weren't buying anything, we ought to leave. Thinking back now, I realize that our desire to speak French had more to do with the fantasy of being seductive and beautiful and mysterious and less to do with the actual language. And truth be told, I was terrible at learning French in school— even though I studied it all the way into high school.

During the summer before my senior year of high school, I read an article in *Mademoiselle* magazine about women's rights and women's liberation. We were into the 1970s now and everything had changed. I was wearing ripped jeans to school and an army jacket covered in protest buttons. One afternoon, I cornered my grandmother on the couch and I told her she should stop letting my grandfather dominate and exploit her. I told her he was oppressing her! Why should she be the one who prepared most of the meals and washed the dishes? Why should she have to jar all those vegetables?

"But, we do it together" was her response. Still, I persisted. "Why do you have to go to the beauty parlor and get dressed up all the time? Grandpa doesn't spend that much time on looking good for you." I moved closer to her and continued. "And why do you always wear skirts and dresses and stockings with heels?"

My grandmother just smiled. She toyed with the pearls around her neck and then asked my mother for a cup of tea. This was her signal that she no longer wanted to have this conversation and the subject was closed.

Nonetheless for me, her response only added to my grandmother's mystery and the mystery of being a French woman.

After graduating from college, I traveled to France. I was twenty-one and thought, *well, now I'll get it.* I interviewed for a dress designer in Paris and did very well taking dictation (it was a British company and they spoke English), but when I sat down to transcribe my notes, I discovered that the European keyboard was just a little bit different than the British and American keyboard. The *a* and the *q* were switched. The period was not in the right place and the *z* was where the *w* was supposed to be! Still, I struggled through. I went to the Alliance Française. I stayed in a fifth floor garret on the Boulevard St. Mitchel with a British girl named Maureen Reardon whom I had met on the channel crossing from Dover to Calais. I met a boy. I fell in love. I fell out of love. I walked through the Jardin du Luxembourg every morning. I mangled the French language and I remained an outsider, a tourist. By February the following year, Paris was cold and rainy. I came down with the flu. I ran out of money. I waited at the American Express office for emergency cash from my parents.

And then I left for London and the comfort of the English language.

SINCE THEN, years have gone by and I have visited France many times over. Still, the country and French women in particular remained a puzzle to me. After my grandmother and my mother died, I was left with many questions about culture, language, history, and how to carry on some remnant of my French ancestors in this big country of ours. I also had so many questions about love and marriage. Both my mother and my grandmother had tumultuous and passionate marriages, but how they kept their husbands fascinated and focused was beyond me. I knew it wasn't about just being "nice" and giving their man exactly what he wanted—in fact, at my mother's funeral, my father got up and spontaneously sang the old song "Thanks for the Memories" for my mother that went: *"you may have driven me crazy, but you never were a bore."*

I am divorced and recently remarried, and so I am particularly interested and invested in the idea of discovering the secrets to how French women keep love alive and constantly intriguing. There are so many things about romance, sex, marriage, and being a woman that my grandmother and mother never had the chance to tell me. This is why I made the decision to travel to France, talk to French women, learn all I could, and then write this book, so that all my American friends can benefit from the lessons French women have to offer.

However, with my lack of language skills, how was I to write a book revealing French women's secrets to getting and keeping love? Despite brushing up with the Pimsleur Language Program audio CD (wonderful, by the way), I needed some help with translating discussions on the delicacies of lingerie and the boudoir confessions. And I needed someone who knew real French women—French women (married and single) who would open their hearts and doors to me.

Enter Jessica Lee. Jessica Lee is a great friend. She is the editor of *New American Paintings*. She is beautiful and she is brilliant. She knows how to dress. She knows exactly where to get your brows done and how to plan a really fun dinner party. She gracefully maneuvers her way through Boston and Cambridge and she is delightfully flirtatious and friendly. As an editor, she travels around the world to art fairs—Basel, Miami, San Francisco, Chicago, and of course she has traveled all over Europe.

She's very educated. Barnard. Her French is impeccable.

Jessica is in her mid-thirties and single. She's an adventurous gal.

And so, off we went to France. Jessica was my translator, my ambassador, and my passport into the country of French women.

We were both transformed by the lessons we learned from the French women we interviewed.

In fact, upon leaving France for Italy, Jessica met a handsome Frenchman at the airport. They sat next to each other on the plane ride. Inspired by the interviews with French women, Jessica chatted with Nelson and, well, sparks flew. Before parting ways, they exchanged information. To this day, they correspond and indeed his recipe appears in this book. Then, another man—a British-Italian—insisted on helping her with her luggage all the way to Florence. Finally, on her way back to America, she had a six-hour layover in London. Jessica needed to get from Gatwick Airport to Victoria Station where she planned to meet her friend Carlo for drinks. She had switched from her usual jeans to a skirt and boots (a very French ensemble). As she stood at the ticket machine, trying to figure out which ticket to buy (zone 1, zone 2, zone 1 and 2, day, week, etc.) she turned to ask a woman for help. While she listened to the woman's explanation, a man walked up beside her and asked, "Do you need help?" He was a Hugh Jackman look-alike. Very British. Very good-looking. Jessica explains it this way:

He came over and just took one of my two bags and started walking toward the escalator. It was a bit awkward, as I had just asked the blond woman who had been helping me if I could follow her to the train. She got on the escalator, then I stepped on, and then a few people and then the man with my bag . . . so, I was looking forward and back, not knowing to whom I should give my allegiance . . . But, well, he had my bag, and then when the train pulled up, she went one way, and he went the other, and I thought, "Well, he is a handsome man, AND he has my bag . . ." so I followed him.

We chatted and laughed, and he asked me for my email just as we pulled up to his stop.

Voilà!! Oh, yes, and each time I was wearing that ensemble of top+denim skirt+boots. I guess it's guaranteed to attract men to help you with your bags!

And upon her return to the States, Jessica received this email from our hero:

. . . was lovely to meet you, albeit too briefly, on the train today. It's a shame you were just traveling through, as I would have loved to have spent more time chatting. Although I do feel somewhat guilty about steamrolling the lady who was being helpful to you onto the sidelines! I guess nature dictates that nothing gets between a man and a very pretty girl in need of some assistance . . .

Just as a sidebar, there really is something to wearing a skirt and boots, especially while traveling. French women are all about that combination. And through our casual research we found that wearing a skirt is much more likely to inspire a man to hold doors open, help with luggage, smile and, yes, chat you up.

AND FOR ME—the married gal? Well, I came home to my husband with a suitcase full of new lingerie, recipes, a deeper understanding of the abiding nature of love, and of course lots of notes, photographs, interviews, and recordings for *French Women Don't Sleep Alone*.

The French women did more than simply provide secrets to love and delicious recipes, they offered me a key to unlock my own past and my relationship with my grandmother. And for this, I will be forever grateful.

Whoever said the French are not a friendly people simply don't know the French. I found them extraordinarily friendly, sensitive, and generous. This was the case in Paris—where Sylvie was our host, through Burgundy, to Besançon (where Jessica and I stayed with Marie-Joëlle and her family) and then up to the north of France, to Lille and Morbecque. We hosted "French Girl Parties" in restaurants and clubs and in private homes. We asked questions to women and men on the street, in cafés and in bars. We met with anyone who was willing to talk to us about the secret to how French women find and keep love. We took photos and recordings of our interviews with French women from eighteen to eighty—women from all socioeconomic categories, urban and rural, working class and university educated. We also talked to American women who have lived in France for many years and French women who now live in America.

Throughout all these meetings, a composite emerged, out of which came this book.

Truthfully, I knew many things about French women on an intuitive level—such as their uncanny ability to maintain a bit of mystery, their coquettish nature, and their sense of discretion when it comes to love, but there were many things I didn't know about until I returned to France for this book. Through my meetings, it was as if I was given back a piece of my own history that had been there inside me all along, but had somehow been misplaced. The experience helped me locate the part of my heart that is one hundred percent French.

After writing this book, I have come to believe it is possible for any American girl or woman to rediscover her own French self—that version of herself that is elegant and discreet, sexy, mysterious, intriguing, charismatic, and charming.

Do note, this is an *idealized* version of "The French Woman." Obviously the French people are individuals and they are all different. Oh, and please take into account that I have a major crush on French women. What is presented here is a composite, an amalgam if you will, that is meant to inspire and help American women create their own version of "The Perfect French Woman."

And while I am suggesting we adopt French women's ways when it comes to love, this is not to say we should turn the clock back to the 1950s and collectively give up our careers, our individual rights, and stay home. This book is about simply borrowing some of the lovely things that work for French women, and incorporating them into our American lives. It's about borrowing the good, only the good.

Consider the French women described in this book as

a metaphor for a way of living that can help us make our love lives more thrilling, sexy, romantic, epic, tantalizing, powerful, and yes, more *satisfying*. Take from this what you will and make it your own. Perhaps you'll find you're a little French, after all.

CHAPTER ONE

﹏

French Women Don't Date

The Great American Date

EVER SINCE YOU WERE a little girl, watching your sister get her hair done in preparation for the prom, waiting at the foot of the stairs for the doorbell to ring, for her date to arrive—you've been busy dreaming about this moment. For you, this first date is a coming of age. You start out as an ordinary girl, playing soccer, getting your knees dirtied, grabbing a bite of pizza on your way to piano practice, and then one day, you suddenly disappear into your bedroom and then just as suddenly, reappear. You are no longer that little girl, but now you've become . . . a princess! You are suddenly all grown up, wearing a Chloé dress, a Prada bag, and yes, Manolo Blahnik heels. Your hair looks fabulous. You are wearing cherry-stained lip-gloss and a sweep of black eyeliner. And the fantasy boy? Well, he is suddenly grown up too. No longer the boy next door, he's been transformed into your magical Mr. Prince Charming.

The actual date? Well, maybe, in the end, it wasn't so magical after all. Maybe you ended up at a kegger and getting sick on the neighbor's front lawn, while your Prince Charming was nowhere to be found and your pretty party dress was all in tatters.

Still, despite all this, the fantasy of the date is always with you. And no matter how old you are, you still believe that if you just wait long enough or try hard enough or join the best Internet dating service or go to the right singles resort—your perfect date is out there.

Love Is Not a Job

So, you roll up your sleeves, you get serious and go to work. You research, you read books, and you go to seminars and singles events. You put yourself on a mission. You give yourself a deadline. You say to yourself you must be married by age thirty-five. Or, you simply need to find a boyfriend before that New Year's Eve party. You will use the rule of numbers and ask twelve friends to each give you three names of eligible bachelors. You gird your loins. You will not give up until you've found your man!

As American women, we are ambitious and career-oriented, and many of us will approach our search for love as if we were a recent MBA grad looking for a great job. We will network and get on the Internet and set up as many dates as humanly possible. We believe that if we concentrate and work hard for six months, we will find the right man. At first, we are very industrious and very optimistic. We'll go on tons of dates, tell all our friends to set us up with single male friends. We'll go to every invite that comes up. We'll exhaust ourselves and after all that work, we often end up disappointed. That's because, deep down or maybe not so deep down, we still believe in the myth of Mr. Right. We believe that there is one man out there and he is absolutely perfect and it's just a matter of hunting him down and finding him.

Dating Fatigue Syndrome

Or, perhaps we don't believe in Mr. Right at all. Perhaps we've grown just a little cynical and we think all men are basically frogs and that it is only through our persistent attentions that they can be transformed into princes. As Americans, we have always been a "can-do" kind of people and so as women, sometimes we see our men as projects. We look at our man with all his flaws, and then put him on a self-improvement regime. We take him shopping for a newly upgraded wardrobe, we get him to the right hairdresser. We recommend a hipper cut. Perhaps even a little waxing? We stay up all night at the computer, overhauling his resume, because we really think he should be making a lot more money, and finally we put our man on that low-cholesterol diet.

And then one day, we give up. We just stop, because we're exhausted and fed up and we just can't do it anymore. And we wonder—where did all the magic go?

Why Can't We Be Friends (with Benefits)?

If you are under a certain age, that scenario may not describe you at all. Maybe you've never dated. You only went on the *anti-date*. Truth is, you are too cool to date in the old-fashioned sense. You're a post-modern deconstruction-ist, and you believe that there are really not that many dif-ferences between men and women and girls and boys, and sex is sex, and why shouldn't we all just hang out and have a good time, because, well, who knows what's going to hap-pen tomorrow. The world might just be coming to some kind of cataclysmic ending. So, let's watch that old David Lynch DVD and order up some pizza and get out the vegan chips from Whole Foods, and oh, yeah, if the moods strikes us, let's have a little sex. Or a lot. Or none at all. It doesn't really matter. We're all friends. Sex is fun. Who knows whom we'll partner up with, because it's not like anyone *owns* any-body else. And hey, this way there's no reason to be jeal-ous. It's all good.

THERE IS SOME ADVANTAGE to "hanging out" over the tradi-tional date: we actually get to *know* the man. We see him with our friends. We hang out in our pj's. We share mixed tapes and favorite DVDs and drink cheap beer. We share our colds and secrets. We laugh, we cry together. We kiss. We hook up.

But then one day, our friend with benefits announces to his little group, his faux-family, that he's met a girl! Some-one he's really serious about, someone he could see spend-ing the rest of his life with! And you're shocked and upset and you can't quite believe what you're hearing because you thought one day he would grow up and see you for the magical, mysterious, awe-inspiring creature you really are and want to spend the rest of his life with you!

Problem is, the two of you are way past the magical-mystery phase. Remember, he saw you with that nasty cold?

He knows about that time you stalked your ex-boyfriend. He's watched you eat a pound of fudge. He knows about the C-you got in chemistry. He knows what you look like after a hard night of partying. Honestly, the gig was up long ago.

Hey, but You'll Always Be Friends

Here's the problem with "hanging out." After a while, it gets old. Actually, past the age of twenty-three, it starts getting old. And that's because we eventually grow up and we want more than a hookup, and as old-fashioned as it may sound, we want to find our own true love. We don't want to go from one guy to the next for the next twenty years, each offering us a new notion of what constitutes a great pizza topping.

We want to be with a man whom we can truly get to know, with whom we can develop a deep and passionate relationship. Someone who challenges us, both emotionally and intellectually, and yes, perhaps a man we can marry and have children with one day.

The Yin and Yang of It

Here's the problem with both the traditional American date and the *anti-date*—they cut off our options. On the traditional date, we are confined to a one-on-one evening and sometimes that's the only opportunity to show ourselves to full advantage. We get dressed up, we look our best, we engage in lively banter. We pull out the little stories from our lives that make us sound fun and cute and interesting. But seriously, how well can someone really get to know you under the artificial constraints of the modern date, especially if you've just met this person? And then there's the inherent pressure to become intimate, because let's be honest—this is what the American date is all about. You are given three, maybe five dates before you have to either go to bed or bail out. But, suppose it takes you longer to figure out how you feel about a man? Suppose you want to get to know a man on a deeper level? Suppose you want to know what his friends and family are like? Suppose you'd like to see how he responds under pressure or what kind of mood he gets in when something doesn't go his way? Well then, you just may well be out of luck and what often happens is you are propelled into intimacy with a guy, and forced to stop seeing other men only to find out that this man is completely wrong for you. And then two months later, you are back out there, dating.

Honestly, it's time to get off the dating treadmill. It's too much pressure on us! It cuts off possibilities and it destroys our sense of mystery. Think about it—when you are on a date, a man knows you are in the market. He knows he is being judged as potential boyfriend/husband material. And he is judging you. Are you wife material? Girlfriend material? Roll in the hay material? Perhaps this is why there is so much personal information revealed on these first dates. We are in a hurry to lay all our cards on the table—our past foibles, our dreams and wishes and desires, our childhood traumas, as well as all the stories about ourselves that show us being funny or charming or inventive. All this in a matter of a few hours with someone we may have just met!

The anti-date is certainly not the solution. If we hang out as if we were overly friendly siblings in pj's, we lose our mystery. If we do sleep with a man in our group, the sex will most likely feel a tad bit incestuous. And the whole setup—lounging around each other's homes or dorms or starter-apartments—takes on the tenor of a "starter relationship." Something you do to experience grown-up life in a safe, noncommittal environment. Even if this is what you want for the time being, you have most likely destroyed any possibility that the man/boy in this group will end up being true love/long-term material. That's because the starter relationship is just that—a starter relationship. It certainly doesn't help us put our best foot forward. That's because there is no *art* to it. And this is where French women know a thing or two.

Consider the French Woman

A French woman will certainly develop a group of close friends, but she will not behave like our American anti-dater and hang out in the dorm in her sweats eating pizza and watching Japanese anime all day. She knows that this simply does nothing to add to her allure or mystery. French women who've been to America just don't get our dating system. *"What the hell is it with the American date—it's like an interview!"* This is from a French woman who lived in America for several years and had to endure the American date. Another French woman said, *"Why waste your time with boring dates with him!!!!"*

The Art of the Dinner Party

While American women are up late on Wednesday nights, worrying whether they'll have a date for Saturday night, our French sisters are on the telephone planning Friday night's dinner party and deciding whether they should serve *coq au vin* (chicken in wine sauce) or *magret de canard* (duck breast) for dinner.

Un Petit Subterfuge

The dinner party is a perfect "cover" for a woman who wants to get to know a man better, before she becomes amorously involved. She can show off her intellect, her great cooking skills, her gift for entertaining and lively conversation. Or, she can simply smile mysteriously and be seen in a great dress. Not bad, either.

Typically, the French dinner party plans begin with a conversation. Perhaps Marie-Joëlle meets at a café with her sister Sylvie. She knows a man from Lyon who is visiting Paris. He's a professor, recently divorced and very charming. Wouldn't it be wonderful to ask him to her Friday night soirée? (French women often host dinner parties on Friday or Saturday nights.) And wouldn't it be wonderful if he became a new member of her group. Marie-Joëlle and Sylvie talk about all the details over lunch at the café. And it's true, their lunch can be as long as two hours! On the way back to the office, they tiptoe over the cobblestone streets in heels, pass by the local *patisserie* (pastry shop) and make a mental note to pick up some wonderful *tarte aux pommes* for the upcoming dinner party. Marie-Joëlle's husband, Jean-François, calls to say he'd like to invite his colleague. *Bien sûr*, the more the merrier.

The party includes the mysterious guest from Lyon as well as an assortment of friends and colleagues.

Everyone comes to the party with a sense of "presentation." No, French women do not get dressed up simply because they want to show off or prove they are the most up on the latest fashion. French women thoughtfully put together their ensembles as a form of politesse. For the French, to wear something pleasing to the eye means that they care enough about their friends and family and new acquaintances to make a showing. And isn't it true—when we all strive to be interesting and lively and attractive, we make the world a more pleasant place. A more intriguing place. A more delightful place.

In America, money is everything, but not so in France. *Beauty* is everything. And you can see this from the design of the metro to the statues in the *Jardin des Plantes*. France is a visual culture and a country that adores the feminine. You'll see voluptuous goddesses and heroines lining the walkway to the Louvre. You'll even see beautiful women on their postage stamps!

The Impromptu Dinner Party

Not all dinner parties are formal or planned weeks or even days in advance. Oftentimes, a French woman will decide on a Friday afternoon to have a get-together that evening, and will simply call her friends (always mixed, men and women) and ask them to bring their favorite dish or a bottle of wine. Sometimes, it's as simple as a few email invitations and then the French woman puts together a salad and a pasta dish, and picks up some dessert at her local bakery. Last minute parties can actually be even more fun and delicious because there is very little pressure on anyone and the mood is light and fanciful.

In addition to the impromptu party, French women will often just drop by each other's homes without actually calling first! I know, it sounds shocking and even a little off-putting to American ears. But, in France—especially in the provinces—this kind of unexpected visit is not at all unusual and will generally lead to a little tea party or an invitation to stay for dinner. No, we're not talking about a fancy dinner, but a simple improvised meal that is warm and welcoming and fun.

And in the Beginning . . . There Is Champagne

For the more formal, planned dinner party, our French woman will begin with champagne. In fact, many French will serve only champagne during the first hour. Sometimes, they will not serve any hors d'oeuvres. Certainly, there's no huge platter of cheese and crackers.

Nancy, an American living in Paris, does lots of entertaining at her home. She is a very busy woman. She is married, has two children, and has a thriving professional life. She often has her colleagues and her husband's business partners over for dinner parties. She tells us that her success is all about the details:

> Flowers—need to be chic, nothing cheesy. No hors d'oeuvres . . . poor taste. Idea is not to fill up the guests before the meal. Starter—soup. Elegant. Homemade. All about the presentation. Can do it in advance, easy and cheap.
>
> Main course. Some sort of elegant stew so can be prepared in advance. Ditto for the rice.
>
> Dessert. Individual chocolate fondants. Soooo easy

and inexpensive, but real showstoppers. Garnish with fresh raspberries and expensive raspberry sorbet. Sprinkle some confectioners sugar on top of fondant. (See the next chapter for recipe.)

Coffee and more champagne or liqueurs in the living room, not at the dining room table.

Key is in the pacing . . . maximum must be done beforehand so guests don't wait around. Set table the night before, etc. Must have a seating plan. DO NOT let couples sit near or next to one another. To really jazz things up, after the main course, have all the men pick up their glasses and move over two places. Adds new life/oxygen to the dinner party. Very important that host and hostess make guests feel welcome . . . talk must be directed to the guests.

Spouses/potential suitors are SO impressed by a good hostess. Have to make it appear seamless and fun. Men love women who know how to entertain, as it is a good reflection on them. Again, all about elegance.

Don't you just love her combination of the French elegance and the American can-do attitude! And her ideas are great. When you host a dinner party, lots of things can be prepared ahead of time and do not have to be expensive. So, while her soup may be an old family recipe that really does not involve a lot of labor or a lot of money, it is served in her family china with the good silverware and linen napkins that she bought at a local flea market. The French woman doesn't pack away her good china and reserve it for only special holidays. For her, every day is festive, every day is an opportunity to enjoy the pleasures of good food, friendship, good company, and lively conversation.

And It's Sexy

The secret to making your dinner party lively and sexy is to properly pace things. Try to do as much preparation as possible before the guests arrive. Delegate as many responsibilities as you can. Often, French dinner parties are a version of what we call "potlucks." Friends will bring their special dish and show off for one another. This adds a sense of delicious competition and an additional opportunity to show off their culinary talents.

As a hostess, it's always helpful to be well prepared, so that the evening runs smoothly. French women will set the table the night before and, as Nancy suggests, create some kind of seating plan. This doesn't have to involve little place cards. Simply have an idea of whom you want to sit next to each other and guide your guests to the right place. This way you can avoid ending up with all the women on one end of the table and all the men on the other end. The French woman will make sure that doesn't happen, because after all, she wants to be certain that there's opportunity for that handsome guest from Lyon to meet her cousin Madeleine, *oui?*

ONCE SEATED, she will begin with a delicious appetizer, such as *foie gras* on toast with a tiny layer of liquid honey. Or perhaps she'll simply serve some oysters with a glass of cold *Sancerre* (white wine). If it's wintertime—potato leek soup, homemade of course. The main course might be a stew, which can also be prepared ahead of time. Or perhaps even *lapin à la moutarde maison*—now, don't be shocked—(rabbit in mustard and cream). All this is accompanied by the perfect wine. Finally, dessert might be something like Nancy's individual *fondant au chocolat* (chocolate lava cake), served with fresh raspberries, raspberry sorbet, and a light dusting of confectioners sugar. Oh, and French women do eat dessert. They will truly indulge themselves at a dinner party. However, typically, our French woman will have tiny portions, and perhaps be more cautious in the days before or following the party. But, she will not deny herself this opportunity for pleasure!

Basically, the thing to keep in mind is that the party is *sensuelle*—using all five of the senses—taste, touch, sound, sight, and smell. There will be the aromas and tastes of delicious food, of course, but there will be music, candles, fresh flowers, the subtle brush of knees touching under the table and a kind of elegant casualness that invites conversation and lively discussion. The French bring sensuality as well as artfulness and an attention to details, especially when it comes to the pleasures of eating and conversation, arguing and discussing the events of the day.

It's Not About You

Yes, and even though you may harbor the dream of capturing the heart of one of your male guests, or a longtime member of your group, the dinner party is not about you. It's about your guests and it's absolutely *de rigueur* that you take very good care of them and make them feel welcome. French women know that a lively discussion on a topic about which her friends feel passionately will put them in the best light. She is there to make them feel warm, comfortable, and very stimulated. Her guests should shine. She will make it all appear quite easy and, indeed, fun. And playful.

For example, she won't be dismayed by the little controversy that arises when Pierre-Olivier declares that the Côtes du Rhône is a bit off. And so, the dinner guests drink the Côtes du Rhône and declare that Pierre-Olivier is mistaken. Later, there may be a little incident when Pierre-Olivier, feeling a bit tipsy, touches Sylvie's hand across the table and for a fraction of a second, a passionate glance is exchanged. But, then it mysteriously, temporarily disappears when our hostess brings out the next course.

All This Work, You Might Say

Is this a terrible sacrifice for our French woman? *Non!* Not at all. The French woman knows that a man is attracted to a woman who is an accomplished hostess, who knows how to cook and knows how to entertain elegantly and makes her guests feel great. Men love a woman who can do this, whether she makes everything from scratch or she makes one great dish and fills in with some excellent store-bought delicacies. Again, it's the presentation that matters. The dinner party is a perfect opportunity to show off their skills and impress.

After the French hostess serves her famous chocolate fondant dessert with fresh raspberries and sorbet, she leads the guests to the living room. There is coffee and more champagne and liquors. By now, the conversation has grown heated and sexy and fun. While the French won't talk much about money or work or business affairs, politics is a favorite subject, and so a fresh debate ensues. It turns out that the mysterious man from Lyon actually voted for President Nicolas Sarkozy! *"How could you?"* demands Marie-Joëlle's husband, Jean-François. And so, the heat and conversation rise to a boiling pitch.

Opinions fly, but it is all deliciously passionate, and no one takes these disagreements personally. It is all a matter of exercising one's mind and sense—of logic and ability to debate with wit. And so, the mysterious man from Lyon is not so mysterious after all, and in fact by the end of the evening, he has found an opportunity to let Sylvie know that he finds her very attractive and would like to take a walk with her through the *Tuilleries* the very next day. Oh yes, and this is the alternative to the American date.

Walk the Walk

Yes, the French don't date. They meet in groups. They throw dinner parties. And if they meet alone, it's to go on a walk. Not only is a walk great exercise and visually stimulating, but with a walk, the whole interview nature of an American date becomes a nonissue. No one is spending money, there is no time limit and there is no expectation that one person will get something in return. Plus, it's the perfect way for a woman to keep a man guessing, to keep her intentions private, and to remain a mystery.

With a walk, the French woman is part of the grand

promenade. This is one of the secrets to her confidence. The man hasn't cornered her alone in a dark restaurant where for two and a half hours she is seemingly his and his alone. Rather, he sees her out in the world, wearing something wonderful. And he sees that she is being seen by other men. He is witness to her power. He knows that there is competition. A walk is a wonderful way to get to know someone without feeling as if there is a time limit. With a walk, or sometimes a bike ride, you can even pretend as if there is no romantic interest at all, but just a friendship. Then you can let this friendship bloom in the midst of other walks, until you are ready to turn it into something more.

Numbers Are Exchanged

By the end of the dinner party, in a quiet moment, a man might ask for a woman's phone number. On the other hand, he doesn't really have to, because he knows he can ask the hostess for the number. What a civilized way to get the information! Compare that to a number scrawled on the back of a damp cocktail napkin in a dark bar. Through the dinner party, our French woman has had the opportunity to observe this man in a group—how he presents himself, talks, laughs, interacts with other men, flirts, holds his wine, discusses politics. And now, when he calls her, she knows a lot more about him than he might tell her on a date or on his Internet dating profile.

The Joy of Cooking

Truth is, the real reason French women embrace the culture of entertaining at home probably evolved from a desire to find a man who has been prescreened and who might make an appropriate match. As Americans, we may balk at all this. We may think the idea that we need to find a man with good credentials is a little distressing, but if we are honest, we'll admit that we have our own methods of weeding out inappropriate men. We go to our college reunions, hoping to reconnect with the fellow who was so brilliant at physics. After all, he's our age and he has shared certain life experiences. Or, we join a mountain climbing club, hoping to meet a rugged sort of man. We go to the singles event at the temple or the church, hoping to meet a man who shares our faith.

How can we adopt the French woman's ways and make them work for an American woman? We may not have the time or wherewithal to throw endless dinner parties. We may not even have a huge group of friends we can depend on. We are busy. We work hard. And oftentimes, we are disconnected from our friends and family in this big, wide country of ours. But, it is possible. Start small. Invite a few friends. Have a potluck. All you're doing is hosting a simple dinner party and creating an opportunity to flirt in a safe and comfortable environment—home. These dinner parties are happening all over France every Friday and Saturday night! And there's no reason why Americans can't join in on the fun. This Friday night, throw a dinner party. If you like, cook one dish and ask your friends to bring their own favorites. Arrange to invite at least one new man. Invite a few you already know and get reacquainted with them. Practice your conversation skills. Show off that new dress. To get started, all you need is a little *subterfuge*. An intention. No, this dinner party isn't about tracking down your

Mr. Right, getting to know him in two weeks and then demanding a commitment. Rather, this dinner party is about letting life flow and enjoying yourself. It's about pleasure. Making friends. Flirting. "Filling your sails" with the attention of one or two or three male admirers. This dinner party is the first step on your road to confidence—confidence in being attractive, desired, and admired.

Truly, love is something that happens while you are going about your life, while you are entertaining and laughing, or walking back to work after a long lunch with your sister. Love is something that is unfolding while you are at the market buying some *comté* (cheese) for the evening. Love is something you discover when you look across the table into your husband's eyes as he is pontificating about journalism to his old school friend. Love is watching your best friend make eye contact with the handsome gentleman from your office, whom you invited at the last minute. And love is weaving around you slowly, even at this party, as you say goodnight and close the door. You may feel as if you have not accomplished anything in terms of finding the man of your dreams. But, love is not about closing the deal, or getting a telephone number, or even being asked out on a date. And truth be told, you have accomplished so much more than this. You have tended to your friendships, you have encouraged new relationships, you have fed and nourished your friends and family. You have given them an unforgettably pleasurable experience. You have helped friendships, and family flourish—and yes, perhaps you have even sown the seeds for new love.

French Lessons

THE NEXT TIME a man asks you out on a date, counter with an invitation to a dinner party with a group of your friends. Be sure to invite at least one male acquaintance along with an interesting mix of other people. Be bold and inventive in your invitations. Not just the same old crowd. Now your "date" can see you in the context of your friends and family and community. Perhaps he'll even discover how well you play the piano! This is how you can "show" how wonderful you are in the context of your natural environment, rather than "telling" him about it during the artificial constraint of a two-hour dinner on a restaurant date. And when he asks you out again (and he will), be mysterious and suggest you go for an afternoon walk!

CHAPTER TWO

⟡

The Joy of Cooking

THE MOST WONDERFUL MEALS—whether they are for big dinner parties, or intimate breakfasts for lovers—begin with a shopping list.

A French Man's Shopping List

The following list is from Jan, a French man living in Boston. He made a special dinner for his girlfriend and her parents—whom he was meeting for the first time. What a wonderful way to introduce himself to her family, with the gift of a fine meal.

Jan's Shopping List
Entree: (appetizer)
   soupe de potiron (butternut squash soup)
   crème (heavy cream)
   fromages (cheese)
   oignons (onions)

Entrée :
x - soupe de potiron
x - crème
x - fromage
x - oignons

Plat :
x - magrets de canard
x - pommes de terre
x - ail   x - champignons ?
x - oranges
x - miel
x - haricots
x - poitrine
- ~~thym~~

Fromages : - brie de Meaux
Bread : - Chiabata bread from
Dessert : - tarte aux citrons
x - citrons
x - œufs
x - crème
x - farine
x - sucre (roux)
x - beurre

Plat: (main course)
magrets de canard (duck breasts)
pommes de terre (potatoes)
ail (garlic)
champignons (mushrooms)
oranges (oranges)
miel (honey)
poitrine fumée (bacon)

Fromages: (cheese)
brie de Meaux

Bread:
chiabata bread

Dessert:
tarte aux citron (lemon tart)
citrons (lemons)
oeufs (eggs)
crème (heavy cream)
farine (flour)
sucre (roux) (brown sugar)
beurre (butter)

How a French Man Seduces

Obviously, it's not just French *women* who love to cook and impress their friends, family, and lovers with delicious meals. Yes, men know that the secret to captivating a woman's imagination is through using all five senses, including touch, smell, sight, sound, and especially, taste.

This is what Nelson, a French man, has to say about the connection between lovemaking and *food*:

✦ ✦ ✦

It's true that the French very much love to link seduction with cuisine (cooking/food). This is what we have inherited from the Romans. In the United States, this isn't how it is? You don't open a bottle of wine before making love?

I will give you a masculine point of view of the ideal dinner menu

Appetizer: **Oysters with a glass of** *Sancerre* **(a white wine)**

Entrée: **Magret de canard (You shouldn't serve something heavy like a 2-pound steak)**

> 1½ small [4-ounce] container of light cream [total 6 ounces]
> Salt
> Pepper (from a pepper grinder)
> 1 can of foie gras
> 2 duck breasts (medium size)
> ½ or ¾ pound of cheese ravioli

Pour cream into a pot and warm on low heat, lightly salt and pepper. Cut half of the block of foie gras into cubes and stir into the cream. Mix for 2 to 3 minutes, and reduce the heat slowly. Set mixture aside. Save half the block of foie gras. Slice into the duck breast on the side with the skin and cook in a frying pan, skin side down, then brown for about 5 to 6 minutes, on each side. In the interim, boil water; salt, cook ravioli.

Place your duck on a large plate, the raviolis to one side, and cover with the foie gras sauce. Place a small slice of foie gras that you have saved on each duck breast.

As an accompaniment, a good bottle of wine (Château Chasse-Spleen), for example, is absolutely necessary—it's my favorite wine because it has a hint of chocolate; and it is thus that Baudelaire and Lord Byron called wine.

Dessert: Un fondant au chocolat, some poires Belle-Hélène, or maybe some small macaroons.

A sip of champagne, and to bed!

✦ ✦ ✦

Pretty sexy, don't you think?

The Art of the Entrée

While this might be shocking to American readers, I really did want to include one recipe for rabbit. Don't get me wrong, I love rabbits and I've even had pet rabbits. Still, I have so many fond memories of my grandfather coming home from a hunting trip in the Connecticut woods with fresh wild rabbit. My grandmother created the most wonderful rabbit stew, using vegetables from their garden. The kitchen filled with the aroma and the taste was exquisite. And yes, the French love to eat rabbit! So, here is our rabbit recipe from Sandrine Soulet. She is from Besançon but now lives in San Rafael, California, with her husband who owns the very popular Aroma Café. She also told us this funny story about a French friend in the United States:

✦ ✦ ✦

A French guy who just came to America wanted to cook rabbit for his boss; he could not find any in the shop so he finally went to Petco. He asked for a rabbit and the lady said, which kind? He said, it doesn't matter, as long as there is enough for four people.

Lapin à la Moutarde Maison
(Rabbit with Mustard)

Preparation: 30 minutes

Cooking time: 1 hour

> 1 rabbit
> Some Dijon mustard
> Olive oil or butter
> 2 cloves garlic
> 1 bottle of dry white wine
> 3 bay leaves
> 1 sprig of thyme
> 1 sugar cube
> 1 carrot
> 5 shallots
> Salt and pepper
> 6 ounces of crème fraîche (or light cream)
> Parsley

Cut the rabbit in pieces and lightly brush on mustard. Brown the pieces in a large skillet with olive oil without burning them.

In the interim, chop the garlic and combine with ¾ of the bottle of dry white wine, along with the bay leaves, the thyme, sugar, and the carrot (cut in slices). Place in a pot and bring to a boil.

Set the browned pieces of rabbit aside and keep warm in a covered dish. Add a bit of olive oil to the skillet used to brown the rabbit and brown the shallots cut in rounds. Add the rabbit and pour in the heated wine mixture. Salt and pepper to taste and allow to cook on a low flame for one hour.

In a bowl, mix crème fraîche (or light cream), chopped parsley, and one teaspoon of mustard.

When done, place the pieces of rabbit on a plate and sprinkle with parsley.

Filter the liquid (optional) and incorporate the crème fraîche and the mustard mixture together. Cook one minute without bringing to a boil and coat the rabbit with the finished mixture.

✦ ✦ ✦

A Simple Dish to Make Your Man Happy

And for those of you who want something a little less challenging than rabbit, here is Sandrine's recipe for chicken marinated in wine. She told us it's "a classic dish that usually makes my husband happy."

✦ ✦ ✦

Coq au Vin

Preparation: 30 minutes + 12 hours of marinating

Cooking time: 2 hours, 45 minutes

    1 chicken, around 6 pounds cut in pieces
    1 onion, sliced
    2 carrots, sliced
    1 bottle of red wine

1 bouquet of herbs
3 tablespoons of oil
1 tablespoon of flour
2 garlic cloves
1 shot glass of cognac
2 tablespoons of seasoning with ½ cup of
   water
Salt, pepper, nutmeg
½ cup of bacon, cut
1¼ cups of mushrooms
A few sprigs of parsley
Peppercorns

The day before, put the pieces of chicken in a salad bowl
with the sliced onion and carrots. Sprinkle the red wine
on top. Add the bouquet of herbs and some peppercorns.
Cover. Let marinate for 12 hours in the refrigerator.

The very same day, drain the pieces of chicken and dry
them with paper towels. Filter the marinade. Dry the
vegetables.

Heat oil in a casserole dish. Brown the pieces of chicken
on all sides. Take the chicken out and then put in the
vegetables. Brown them for 3 to 5 minutes. Sprinkle
with flour. Stir it well.

Put the pieces of chicken back in, and add crushed
cloves of garlic. Flame with the cognac.

Pour the wine marinade in with the seasoning bouillon
water. Add salt and pepper and nutmeg. Once boiling,
cover. Let it cook for 2 hours on low.

Fifteen minutes before being served, in a nonstick frying pan, brown the pieces of bacon and the sliced mush-

rooms. Add this into the casserole dish. Season and sprinkle with some parsley.

Serve hot. Makes enough for eight people.

✦ ✦ ✦

Summer Celebrations

This recipe comes from Carol Merriman, who spends every summer in the Ardeche, in southern France. Her recipe for a wine drink is similar to sangria, except it's made with white wine. The French serve it at parties to celebrate the summer fête, les Feux de la Saint-Jean. This is a festival to celebrate the summer solstice on June 21. As part of the pagan fertility rite, all the marriageable men in a village take turns jumping over a bonfire. Whoever makes the leap will supposedly be married within the year. Nowadays, the marriageable young women also jump. They do this until the fire dies down and then the children jump over the bonfire. This is a wild and fun celebration and is sometimes followed by a DJ playing music for dancing.

✦ ✦ ✦

Marquisette

Two liters of white wine (usually sparkling)
¼ bottle of rum
Half a liter of seltzer water
2 lemons, cut into slices
2 oranges, cut into sliced
2 apples, chopped
1 cup of sugar

✦ ✦ ✦

Carol Merriman's French friend Béatrice lives in Toulouse. She lost her first husband when he was thirty-six and raised their two sons (now teenagers) alone. A few years ago, she visited a childhood friend whom she had not seen in almost forty years. Well, sparks flew and they have been dating ever since. Béatrice and her boyfriend have a long-distance relationship, but whenever he visits, she always cooks something wonderful. The following is a recipe she offered us:

✦ ✦ ✦

Strawberries with Szechwan Pepper and Basil

Wash, drain, and remove stems from a quart of strawberries. Slice or quarter the strawberries. Sprinkle with Szechwan pepper (about five twists of the pepper mill) and 5 tablespoons of sugar. Add 7 or 8 chopped basil leaves.

Serve immediately or chill for three hours in the refrigerator (cover with plastic wrap).

✦ ✦ ✦

Happy Birthday Dinner

Myriam Aouadi is a fabulous cook and we're lucky to have her entire menu for her boyfriend's birthday dinner. She was born in a small city in the Provence region of France called Fréjus, and moved to Nice for college where she received her Ph.D. This is when she started cooking for her friends and boyfriends. She lives in Cambridge, Massachusetts, now.

When we asked her about how she started cooking, this is what she told us:

> Actually, I don't know how I learned how to cook, but my mother is a wonderful cook and I was always around her when I was a little girl, trying to do the same thing. She was using a lot of different spices that she was preparing and mixing by herself. All the colors, the fragrances, and also the texture when she was showing me how to prepare bread ... she is way better than me! I think that it's also a pleasure to cook when you do your own grocery shopping, especially when you have access to outdoor markets or small shops. For instance, when I was in France, I liked to go sometimes to Italy [15 minutes from Nice by car], to buy some Bresaola [a kind of dried beef].
>
> Concerning food and love, I just think that cooking for someone you appreciate just shows that you care about her/him and you want to please her/him. Nobody can be indifferent to that. . . . But I also like to explain what I cooked during the meal, that's also the sensual part. I mean, how you choose the ingredients, how you cooked them and why. When you see someone having some pleasure eating something that you cooked, it also gives you some pleasure. The presentation is also important. So first you have the pleasure of the fragrance, then the pleasure of the eyes, and finally the taste. A little caress on the hand while you describe your recipe—and all the senses are awake! Another thing I enjoy is to cook together.

Why I prepared this menu?

First, it depends on the person. For instance, my boyfriend is French, so I know that I can use foie gras. He has been in the U.S. a few months, so I thought it would be nice to use some French ingredients and to prepare a wonderful dinner so he will feel like home. The mix with salty and sweet and crunchy and soft—for the sensations, but also because he told me he liked to be surprised—and the chocolate because he told me he liked it and because it's an aphrodisiac and sensual.

Actually, I try not to think about what menu I want. I think about one thing: the appetizer or the entrée and from that I go grocery shopping. I start to cook and I'll go with my feelings thinking about how the dinner will go.

It's true, the way to a man's heart is through his stomach.

And now, Myriam's dinner menu:

✦ ✦ ✦

Appetizer: Foie gras sur lit de miel (foie gras honey toast)

> **Whole wheat sliced bread**
> **Liquid honey**
> **Foie gras**
> **Salt and cracked pepper**

Preheat oven to 350 degrees F. Line each slice of bread with a layer of liquid honey and add a slice of foie gras. Bake for 5 to 10 minutes, until the foie gras melts and

the bread is crusty. Season with salt and cracked pepper.

Entrée: Caramelized onion beef served with mango-eggplant sauté

> 1 big onion
> 1 teaspoon of canola or sunflower oil
> 2 teaspoons of white sugar
> Beefsteak (0.5–0.7 pound)
> 1 mango
> 1 eggplant
> 3 teaspoons of olive oil
> 3 teaspoons of crushed hazelnuts or almonds
> Salt and pepper

Slice onions into ¼-inch-wide rings. Heat sunflower (or Canola) oil. Add onions and slowly cook over medium heat, stirring often (for 15 to 20 minutes). Add the sugar and cook until onions are caramel colored (10 minutes).

Cut the beef in small pieces and cook (without oil) as you like it. Add the caramelized onions and cook for 2 to 3 minutes.

Cut the mango and the eggplant in small pieces. Heat the olive oil and cook the eggplant over medium heat for 15 minutes. Add the mango and cook slowly over medium heat for 20 minutes. Stir often but carefully to avoid crushing the pieces. Add the crushed hazelnuts or almonds, the salt, and the cracked pepper. Cook for 2 more minutes.

Dessert: Banana chocolate ganache pie with whipped cream

> 1 banana

FOR THE CHOCOLATE GANACHE:
   9 ounces of dark chocolate
   5 ounces of heavy cream

FOR THE PASTRY:
   8 ounces unsalted butter, softened
   ¾ cup confectioners sugar
   2 teaspoons pure vanilla extract
   2 cups all purpose flour
   1 teaspoon salt
   (or you can use a store-bought pie crust)

FOR THE WHIPPED CREAM:
   3.5 ounces of whipping cream
   2 teaspoons of confectioners sugar

Heat oven to 375 degrees F.

FOR PASTRY:

Cream butter and sugar until pale and fluffy, and mix in vanilla. Add the flour and the salt, and mix until just combined and crumbly (do not overmix). Pat the dough into a disk, and wrap in plastic. Refrigerate for at least 1 hour. Unwrap and roll out dough and place tart shell in pie pan. Make holes using a fork.

FOR THE GANACHE:

Melt dark chocolate with 2 teaspoons of water; add 5 ounces of heavy cream and cook 5 minutes over medium heat while stirring. Cover the pastry with a layer of banana slices and a layer of chocolate ganache. Cook in the oven for 20 minutes. Place in the refrigerator after cooling for at least 2 hours.

FOR THE WHIPPED CREAM:

For the whipped cream, everything has to be cold: place the bowl and the beaters of an electric mixer in the freezer and take them out just before using them. Mix (high speed) the whipping cream with the sugar.

Serve the pie with some whipped cream on the side and you can also add a strawberry for the pleasure of the eyes!

With the entrée, you can have some red wine (I served some Châteauneuf du Pape) and of course champagne for the dessert!!!

✦ ✦ ✦

For Everyday *Joi de Vivre*

Even if you don't like to do a lot of cooking, and really are all thumbs in the kitchen, there are simple ways to make charming meals. Look for fresh foods, rather than frozen, canned, or processed. Choose seasonal fruits and vegetables. And contrary to the myth of the Meat and Potatoes Man, men love vegetables. Here's what Julie Salaber from Paris says:

> I like cooking vegetables, in any season. Men often don't know how good vegetables can be when well prepared!
> But I don't really follow any proper recipe.
> During the summer, I make a lot of mixed salads, with many colors: pasta, tomatoes, cucumber, lettuce, corn, ham, and mozzarella. I cut all the ingredients into small pieces, and add some mayonnaise in the dressing!

During the winter, I cook vegetable soups with potatoes, carrots, onions, leeks, and a cube beef bouillon. I just put everything in boiling water and cook over low heat. As you may notice, I can't give you a recipe because I just cook following my mood—and what I have in my fridge!

A Dessert to Make You Swoon

The following chocolate mousse recipe came to me from Stéphanie Desprat, a French woman from southwestern France, although she spent her childhood in a little village called Soturac. She is currently living in Cape Cod. She's a climate change scientist, researching pollen found in marine sediments, and while she has adopted many of our American ways, she retains her essential Frenchness. She wears fabulously fashionable clothes, and great boots—even though most of the scientists at the Oceanographic Institute wear sneakers and Birkenstocks. And of course, she loves to cook! When I asked if I could interview her, she invited me to come to her house for lunch. I arrived to find Stéphanie and another French woman scientist busy at the stove, creating an aromatic meal of fresh fish, vegetables, and crusty bread. We got to talking about love, romance, marriage, and then food. Here is her recipe for chocolate mousse.

(For 1 or 2 persons)
1 tablespoon of sugar
1 egg
1.5 ounces dark chocolate
1 pinch of salt

Beat sugar with egg yolk until it goes white.Chop chocolate in pieces and melt it using the double boiler method (bain-marie). Mix up melted chocolate with the egg yolk and sugar preparation.

Beat the egg whites (plus pinch of salt) until really stiff. Add the egg whites very gently to the chocolate preparation.

Fill ramekins (small baking dishes). Let cool down in the fridge during 3 to 4 hours. And it's done!

Tricks and Tips from Stéphanie

+ I always use "Nestlé Chocolat coarse"—it is a chocolate for cooking with 64 percent cacao. It is probably possible to find an equivalent here in the U.S.

+ For 2 persons the amount is small, it is better to double the proportions.

+ We can add a tablespoon of butter, or rum, or Grand Marnier or whatever flavor you like (my favorite is with a bit of Grand Marnier but I generally prefer when the taste of dark chocolate is not masked by other flavors).

+ The chocolate mousse goes very well with strawberries. We do a dessert called "*verrines de mousse au chocolat*": just before eating the mousse, we can add on the top the chocolate mousse crunchy crumpled cookies (for example, Bordeaux cookies from Pepperidge Farm are perfect for that) and above, some strawberries. For this dessert we can put the chocolate mousse preparation before cooling in beautiful glasses, so you will see the different layers . . . it is beautiful and excellent!

More Chocolate!

Remember my friend Nancy and her fabulous Parisian dinner parties? Her chocolate fondant (lava cake) is her signature recipe and she has generously offered it to our American readers.

✦ ✦ ✦

Chocolate Fondant (Lava Cake)

Yield: 10 servings

> 7 ounces semi or bittersweet chocolate
> (preferably 70% cocoa), chopped coarsely
> 1 stick of butter
> 4 eggs
> ½ cup sugar
> 2 tablespoons of all-purpose flour
> ¼ teaspoon salt
> 1 teaspoon vanilla extract

1. Preheat oven to 400 degrees F.
2. Butter individual ramekins and dust inside with loose flour (throw out excess flour).
3. Break the chocolate into small pieces and melt it in a double boiler with butter over hot water.
4. Beat the eggs with sugar and mix with flour and salt.
5. Slowly fold in the melted butter and chocolate. Add vanilla extract.
6. Ladle into ramekins. Place on cookie sheet. Can be covered lightly with plastic wrap and kept on cookie sheet in refrigerator for up to 8 hours. During dinner

party, remove 30 minutes prior to baking. Bake while
guests are eating the main course.

7. Bake at 400 degrees for approximately 12 minutes;
the outer part should be cooked and the inner part
liquid.

The chocolate fondants (left in the ramekins and served
on top of an individual plate) should be served hot with
a light dusting of confectioners sugar. Very elegant to place
raspberries on the side along with a spoonful of raspberry
sorbet. Showstopper.

Variations

+ You may add two tablespoons of orange liqueur and
finely grated rind of one orange. This gives a delicious
orange-chocolate flavor.

+ You may try adding some ground cinnamon and nutmeg
or cloves to the chocolate and butter mixture.

+ You may add some mint flavoring.

+ You may add a little coffee essence to mixture.

✦ ✦ ✦

Berries Galore

Margaret Brooks is an American who teaches French and
is a total Francophile. She now lives in Connecticut, but she
lived in France for many years and is a wonderful cook.
She was generous enough to offer us her recipe for Berry
Clafoutis, which can be served as a breakfast with coffee,

or as a dessert. Here's what she told us about these delicious muffin-like treats:

✦ ✦ ✦

It's interesting that in France they don't take the pits out of the cherries! I think the word *clafoutis* is from the Limousin and the berry area of France; the word may be of African origin. I think that when it's for breakfast, it's a little more pancakey; for dessert, it's more custardy.

✦ ✦ ✦

Berry Clafoutis

2 eggs
⅓ cup sugar
½ teaspoon vanilla extract
3 tablespoons flour
Pinch of salt
⅔ cup crème fraîche (you can buy this French
    cream or make it by mixing ordinary cream
    with sour cream (half and half) and letting
    it stand awhile)
⅓ cup milk
One pint berries—raspberries, blackberries,
    whatever—or sliced peaches or cherries or
    sliced pears.

Heat oven to 400 degrees. Butter a 10" round baking dish or pan. Whisk eggs with sugar until thick; add vanilla; add flour and salt. Mix half the crème fraîche with the milk and whisk into batter. (Save the rest of the crème frâiche.) Pour ⅓ of batter into the dish and bake for 5 minutes to set; cover with the berries and pour in the rest of the batter.

Bake about 25 minutes until set; remove from oven and cool a bit; sprinkle with confectioners sugar and serve with remaining crème fraîche.

✦ ✦ ✦

Breakfast in Bed from Tania

Tania, a charming woman we met in Paris, sent us this:

A great thing for breakfast in bed is the regular French breakfast with:

- ✦ Fresh baguette with butter and comfiture
- ✦ Fresh croissant, pains au chocolat
- ✦ Fresh squeezed orange juice
- ✦ Tea, hot chocolate, or coffee

I just love having breakfast in bed with my "man," especially when you stay in bed after and make love :-)

If You Love Food, You Love Living

None of these recipes will help you in a quest to lose weight. That's not what this is all about. This is about pleasure and love. And while we may not want to make a habit of eating foods with heavy cream and tons of butter, every now and then, for special occasions, it's really all right.

The notion of showing love through food may have gotten some of us in trouble in the past—certainly as a life-time member of Weight Watchers™, I'm included in that group. However, I have learned that when food is treated with respect and joy, we receive so much pleasure and we give pleasure. This is not a crime and there is usually nothing sinister about someone who wants to give you the gift of a delicious meal or a *to-die-for* dessert. I believe that we get into trouble with food when we get into an adversarial relationship with it. Rather than battling with food, why not befriend it? Why not get to know an egg? Get cozy with the vegetables? Become acquainted with good, dark chocolate? Say hello to bread? Wink at the cheese?

After a while, there will be fewer clandestine midnight meetings in the food pantry. The desire to ravish a bag of chips will dissipate. Why? Because, when we become really good friends with food, and we introduce these food friends to our loved ones, we are no longer keeping food as our secret lovers. Rather, we are making our lovers . . . our lovers. And food takes its proper place in our hearts and lives. Food becomes simply food, something that enhances our relationships, brings joy and satisfaction and yes, provides us a way to *show* our love.

French women have known this for years. Julie Salaber told us this:

> I love eating, and I think men prefer girls who eat rather than girls who are on a diet. If you love eating, you love living!!!

So, begin living now. Really living. And loving.

The French Girl's Version of the Bag of Chips

Despite the fact that I've done all this research and started cooking more and cut all the salty, sugary, processed foods out of my life, I will say this: I miss those days when I would mindlessly eat out of a bag. There is something incredibly satisfying about the seemingly limitless quantity in a bag and the sense that this big bag is mine and mine alone. Perhaps this is an American thing, from the days when we were pioneers moving West all looking for a piece of our own land, far from the neighboring farms. Or perhaps it's from my childhood and the days when my mother would appease me with a box of Ritz Crackers. (I still have strong memories of crying on the back porch of our house, clutching a box of those salty/sweet crackers while my parents fought inside the house.)

I assumed French women would never eat out of a bag. However, on a recent trip to Paris, I saw just that. Yes, I saw young French women on their lunch break, having a kind of picnic on one of the bridges across the Seine. It was a lovely sunny day and two women were eating out of plastic bags. I came closer and I realized that these were not bags of chips, but bags of cut-up lettuce—fresh baby greens! Ah, the French . . .

I've tried this at home by buying a bag of greens, spraying on a bit of natural olive oil, and adding some salt and freshly ground pepper. It's amazingly satisfying! I get the experience of something that is in a bag—all mine! And, it's salty and crunchy and very, very healthy.

Food Is Love

Don't think the French are without a sense of whimsy. When I asked Havoise, a beautiful young French woman who recently moved from Pas-de-Calais to Paris, for a "recipe for love," she wrote that she had none, but later she sent this poem, saying *"I think I have invented a recipe for you"*:

by Havoise Mignotte

Take a chicken
Cook it in the oven
Just the way you like it
The way you prefer
No matter if it's garlic
No matter if it's new
Just love what you do

You'll eat on the table
You'll eat on the floor
You'll eat where you want to
Who matters what you do

I would not forget a bottle of wine
But the only thing to have
is your smile in your eyes
And your smile on your face
Your smile in your body
And your smile on your hands
Do you understand me?

Then drink the moment
Oh please be selfish
Please be really you
And feel how good it is
When nothing bothers you
When everything's so light
And you do what you do

Then eat that chicken
Well cooked or burnt
Stay there, go away
And do it every day.

French Lessons

INVITE A FEW FRIENDS over for dinner. Choose a few recipes and write a shopping list. Next, go to your market and buy the best, most fresh ingredients. Take time making your meal. Enjoy the sensual details and enjoy your party.

If you are the type to eat less-than-healthy foods alone, then fill your house with really delicious, fresh foods. Banish the processed and pre-packaged foods. Start cooking for yourself and eat with a sense of conscious pleasure. Set the table with real china and silverware. Eat with friends and loved ones whenever possible (never while reading or in front of the TV!). Eat slowly and eat one food at a time. And as Mireille Guiliano suggests in *French Women Don't Get Fat*, try putting each individual portion on the center of a different dish and serving them one at a time. This is what French women do and it really helps if you're trying to slow down eating and appreciate all the individual textures, aromas, and flavors.

Finally, stop dieting, and (as Weight Watchers™ says) start living!

CHAPTER THREE

~

Meeting Men . . . C'est Facile!

WHEN ASKED WHERE SHE MEETS MEN, our French woman laughed and often said, simply, *"anywhere!"* She meets men at university, in bars with friends, at nightclubs, in the metro, the market, at cafés—while reading a book, at parties, at her work. Everywhere. All the French women we spoke to described how whenever they left the privacy of their own home, they got dressed up. They all had an attitude of *"well, you never know what could happen."* And every French woman we spoke with talked about the chance meeting. The sudden connection. The shared moment. Lively conversation is a national pastime in France and so our French woman will get into discussions with the man at the Brix, the wine store, or while she is renting a bike in Paris or simply looking for a good film to see. She always goes out with the possibility that she might meet a man while buying bread or going to the library. She leaves her house wearing a pair of great-fitting jeans, boots, a very cool jacket, and perhaps a vintage messenger bag.

Butterflies Are Free

Or it might happen like this: the French woman brings a book on the study of butterflies to her local café. She's honestly interested in butterflies, but she knows if she sits at home and reads, she will not meet anyone. At the café, yes, a man notices her. He asks about the book. Butterflies? She tells him what she has learned about them—most butterflies will only live for about two weeks after they emerge from the chrysalis. And in that short amount of time, they must find a mate before they die.

How sad! How moving! And yes, there are beautiful photographs in this book. It's a veritable fashion show of butterflies in brilliant jewel-like colors! She shows this to our gentleman and he is enthralled.

The waiter delivers her *citron pressé* (lemonade) and then there is a moment. In the context of talking about butterflies, our French woman gets to know this man a little bit. Perhaps she will invite him to join her friends tonight at the bar where they always congregate. Or perhaps she is not interested in anything further than this brief conversation. The French woman knows that while this talk over pictures of butterflies takes place, there are other men noticing her. All this attention conspires to make our French woman feel desirable and very confident. And confidence is the key to the French woman's power.

French women generally don't believe in love at first sight, but they are open to the possibility. One French woman said, *"It's rare that it's love at first sight. First we meet, and then we become friends, and then perhaps an attraction develops."* She knows that every man she meets might be a potential lover or simply a friend, or perhaps just someone who makes her feel desirable, and that's all. There is no end game, just a natural flow. Still, another perhaps more cynical French woman said this:

> As soon as a man says he loves you, it's absolutely not true. A good man will not tell you he loves you right away. After a month it's impossible for a man to be in love with you and want to spend his life with you and have children with you. There's no such thing as love at first sight.

Dress for Success, French-Style

When you ask a French woman how she met her boyfriend, she will pause a moment and look confused. How *did* she meet him? This is because meeting men is simply a part of her everyday life. She doesn't really make an effort. She is simply present. She is simply herself.

Nonetheless, she does wear clothes that make her feel confident and always good lingerie—every day. She wears this for her*self*. French women treat dressing as an art form. They love to create their own unique ensembles. This is what she was brought up to do and it's her lifelong passion.

To be fair, many French women tell us that fashion is different in France. One young woman who now lives in America told us that she found the clothes in France to be more feminine, with more styles in more affordable price ranges. She felt it was easier to find her own style back home and now that she's living in America, it's a bit of a challenge. She often shops in New York City, gets her basics locally, and mixes in unique and interesting pieces she finds in consignment shops. The French have a long tradition of discovering treasures in flea markets and secondhand shops. And think about it, isn't it good for our environment? One woman's fashion disaster could be another woman's new signature accessory.

So, while it may not be quite as easy for Americans to dress artfully, especially on a budget, it is possible, if we are willing to be inventive.

We're All Busy

As Americans, we live in an incredibly busy world and we all have a lot of responsibilities. We have our careers, our families, and our homes. We go to the gym. We go out with friends. We have our book clubs and our yoga classes. We have a million errands to run. And then there's all that email to answer and gifts to buy and shopping to be done. And we think, I want to find love. Or, I want to make my relationship or my marriage better. More romantic. Sexier. More fun. But, I haven't got the time to worry about it. In fact, we often think of romance, love, and meeting men as some kind of chore or appointment, just as we think of exercise as something we do three days a week at the gym and not something we integrate into our everyday lives.

But, our French sisters manage to integrate it all into their everyday lives. They get exercise by walking everywhere, or biking, and carrying their groceries. They don't understand the necessity of stopping their lives to go to a gym. And besides, they say, it doesn't sound like much fun.

They feel the same way about love. For them, even the search must be pleasurable and it must be part of their everyday lives. There's no "stop and start."

The eBay of Love

When we've yet to learn how to integrate meeting men, being social, and having fun into our everyday lives, we get frustrated and a little annoyed. It seems like so much trouble to find a companion and a lover. We don't want to sleep alone, but we don't want to stop our whole lives in order to go on a quest for love. Still, in our earnest efforts to find love, we often turn to the Internet and online dating services. We treat love and meeting men like another chore or a job or a little cottage industry. We go "shopping" for our lovers, our boyfriends, our potential husbands. We put up profiles and wait for the offers to come in. And they do come in. In fact, sometimes it can feel like the eBay of Love, only there's generally no space for people to truly recommend the integrity of this person, this potential lover who is there online, selling you something much more important than the faux leopard jacket that Kate Moss made popular. And what about that photograph that turns out to be ten years old? Oh, and the latest discovery—some men actually lift other men's profile essays, so they are completely misrepresenting themselves. It is no surprise that often, when we finally meet a man through a service or outside the context of our work and family and friends, we end up—at the very least—not really connecting. And in the worst-case scenario, we end up having to change our email address and ignore the plaintive missives from an unwanted suitor.

It's true, some French women do use online dating services, but it is not nearly as popular as it is here in the United States. This is because French women don't parse out the aspects of their lives the way we do. For a French woman, every moment of the day and every activity is an opportunity to enjoy the sensual pleasures of life. That's the key, really, because French women are less likely to "turn it on" and then "turn it off." For a French woman, all of life is romantic and sensual and pleasurable. They are always ready for seduction.

So How Do French Women Meet Their Boyfriends and Husbands?

France is a small country. Add to this their deeply engrained belief in the value of a good education and you'll find that many French men and women meet their future partners in school or at university. Many end up marrying the boy or girl they were friends with as children. Oftentimes, the families have known each other for generations. And in certain societies, parties are organized to introduce young women to young men of similar social status.

Of course, not every French woman meets her husband or boyfriend as a child or at university or through organized parties. But, this way of meeting through family and friends and through common interests is an important part of the social structure. And so, if a French woman hasn't met her man through these avenues, she might meet him at her job.

And yes, there is a lot of on-the-job fraternizing going on and it's not at all frowned upon the way it is in America. In fact, the French are quite amused by our zealousness when it comes to sexual harassment lawsuits. One French man told us how before he came to work in America, his friends teasingly warned him not to get into an elevator alone with a woman in the States or he could get sued for sexually harassing her. He was very careful not to flirt or say anything personal, even a compliment, for fear that it might be misinterpreted.

Fraternizing on the Job

Our American men are very nervous about their behavoir on the job. In their earnest attempts not to get into trouble with their human resources departments, they will go out of their way to ignore the fact that there is a difference between men and women. American men will strive to treat us as exactly the same, pushing any thoughts of sexuality out of their minds while on the job. And while we appreciate the possible legal ramifications, and we do want equal pay for equal work and to be treated as professionals and rewarded for our efforts, there is this gnawing sense that an essential part of our selves is being ignored: the fact that we are *female*. We are different from men.

We strive to be professional at work and we were taught that to be professional we must dress in a gender-neutral fashion. And so, we will dress in a pantsuit and basically adopt masculine attire. And then, later that night when we're out on our American date, we swing in the other direction, because our sexuality has been tightly kept under wraps all week long at our jobs. So we wear a low-cut, mini-cocktail dress with six-inch heels. It's that either/or mentality. And it doesn't serve us.

Reclaiming Femininity

French women never forget they are female. So, whether they are walking in their neighborhood in the 5th arrondissement, or running a business meeting at work, they still maintain a sense of femininity. Not femininity as in pink floral prints, frills, lace, and bows—but femininity as in the quality of *being female.* This is accomplished by wearing basic business attire, with one accessory or detail that subtly reminds the world that she is still a woman. Perhaps she will wear an interesting pin or a sexy skirt with a buttoned up jacket. Perhaps a pair of fabulous high heels with slim pants. She quietly integrates her sensuality into her everyday business wardrobe. French women don't believe in either/or. *"I am a strict business woman!"* or *"I am a sexpot!"*

The Baby with the Bathwater

No, we don't want men to act rude or crude or completely inappropriately, but a little light flirtation, a bit of fun on the job, is not completely a bad thing and it can make life more pleasant. More sexy. And think about it—when you're working, are you not at your best? You are dressed well and you are seen as a capable, accomplished, and even powerful individual. And the men you meet on the job?

You can see them in the context of their real world, how they act with their boss, their coworkers. How do they cope with stress? And certainly the fact that you are in an office and not on a date provides a wonderful way to buy some time, to really get to know a man and decide if you want to take things further. Besides, a little forbidden love and the necessity of secrecy can add a lot of heat to any romance.

French women aren't chastised for wearing something slightly sexy to work. In fact, the French television newscaster Claire Chazal shows off her cleavage every night in France on the evening news at eight o'clock. The French see nothing unusual about it. *"She's a woman. She has breasts. What is the problem?"* they say. In fact, all the female newscasters show a bit of cleavage and no one blinks an eye.

Get to Know Your Man

You might think that living in such a close-knit society would make it difficult to meet men, but actually it's incredibly helpful because the intertwining of relationships between family and community and school provides a kind of screening process or audition, if you will. By the time a French woman meets a man at her cousin's dinner party, he has been completely vetted. He knows her cousin, he has worked with her brother; perhaps he plays tennis at the same club. There are several connecting factors. She is not meeting a stranger; this is not a blind date. He is *known*. This idea of being known is of utmost importance in France.

During a recent visit, I met with my dear friend Margie.

She is an American living in the north of France, and she has kept many of her American habits. In fact, she does not buy her meat at her local *boucherie* (butcher shop), but rather she buys it at the *supermarché* (supermarket.) One day, the postman wanted to deliver a package to her, but she wasn't home. And so, he went to the village *boucherie* near her home and asked to leave the package there for her, assuming she would come by later in the day and they would give her the package then. But, the owner of the shop said, he had never heard of this Margie! The post-man was clearly shocked by this. How could he not know a woman who lived a few doors away? Surely she shopped there! Well, later in the week, Margie did get her package. The postman found her home and when she answered the door and signed for the delivery, he explained to her how he had tried to deliver the box to the *boucherie,* but that this was not possible because they didn't know her name. Margie said she didn't shop there. She was smart enough not to tell him that she preferred the anonymity of the *super-marché,* and simply signed for the delivery. But the post-man shook his head and persisted, "But Madame," he said, "he does not *know you!*" He was still stuck on the fact that the *boucherie* did not know Margie. He repeated himself, *"Il ne vous connaît pas!"* ("He does not know you!")

Why Is Being "Known" So Important?

Community, family, and friendships are crucial ingredients when it comes to finding and keeping love. This is why French women seldom have "girl parties" the way we do. "What's the point?" they ask. "Where's the fun in that?" In preparation for our interviews, we asked to meet with French *women* only and insisted that boyfriends, male friends, and husbands not join us. The French girls simply could not understand this and although they finally agreed to show up alone, after a few hours, the men began arriving. For a French woman, every opportunity to go out with a group of friends to a bar or café or to meet at someone's home is an opportunity for romance, flirtation, and seduction. Men and women truly love each other in France. They admire one another. One woman said to us, *"There is no big tension between men and women here."* She went on to explain how she felt that the women's movement in America created a rift between the sexes, and many arguments about who is cooking, and who is cleaning. The French we talked to seem to really appreciate the difference between the sexes. We spoke to one French man who lived and worked in America for a few years. He was completely confused by how *masculine* some businesswomen in the States appeared.

To BE feminine is a wonderful thing in France. *Féminité* (femininity) is not a dirty word there. Women wear lingerie, perfume, creams, and some natural-looking makeup. They will choose clothes that emphasize their femaleness— their breasts, their long legs, their slender waists. Or, occasionally, they will engage in a little gender-bending fashion and wear a newspaper boy's cap and a pair of laceup boots, perhaps an oversized tweed jacket. This dressing up like a boy is playful and only serves to emphasize their femaleness.

So, when French men and women get together in a group,

there is a delicious sense of possibility. At dinner parties, husbands and wives are seldom seated together. Where's the fun in that, after all? The men do not retreat to the den to watch a soccer game while the women huddle together in the kitchen to discuss their children and the latest report on what five-year-old Sienna did at school today. Rather, everyone mingles. Young and old, single and married.

But, think about it—by socializing this way, French women meet many men and they are able to "show off" their desirability in the context of friends and family. And everyone shows off. It's a national pastime. If you walk down a street in France, particularly in the cities, you will find men and women promenading, wearing great clothes and looking their best.

My American friend Nancy who lives in Paris was very confused by this when she first arrived. *"I couldn't understand why the women seemed to get more dressed up on weekends when they took their children to the park. Why did they wear a skirt and high heels?"* In America, we tend to dress down on weekends, but not so the French. French women take even more care to look good on weekends because their husbands or partners or boyfriends are home and the streets are filled with men and women enjoying their days off. Rather than using the weekend as an opportunity to dress in workout clothes (something the French can't fathom), they dress for show. When I recently interviewed two French women—Ph.D. candidates, staying here in America—they expressed a genuine shock at the way we dress. *"What is this with the pajamas? How can you wear pajamas to work?"* they asked.

They were talking about those flannel pajama pants. You know the ones. They're supposed to be pants, but truthfully, don't they look like pajamas?

This Is Your Life

This French way of living and dressing and caring for oneself might seem like a lot of work. And after all, we do live in a big country. Most of us don't belong to a close-knit community. We don't have time to go to dinner parties or hang out with girls and boys in cafés and stare at each other all day. We have work to do, we say. But consider this—if you're looking for a mate, what are you doing? Checking online sites? Calling fifty friends to set up blind dates? Going to singles events or speed dating? This takes a lot more effort and truthfully, it's not much fun. And it's not really very natural.

And if you're married or live with your partner and you want him to focus more on you—what better way than to show him that you are a woman of the world, stylish and well groomed, and other men are taking notice of you. He won't see this unless you go out in mixed company!

Take a cue from French women and integrate love and romance and beauty into your everyday life. End the cycle of either/or: dressing for a date vs. dressing for the gym. Going out vs. staying in. It's that same mentality that we have with our feast or famine diets. We deny ourselves and then suddenly we are famished and so we overdo things. With love, we deny our sensuality and then we grow anxious and restless and lose our sense of confidence and end up sleeping with some guy who's really not good for us, who is the emotional equivalent of a big bag of chips.

Walk Softly and Carry a Big Book

As an American woman, you can still meet men in the French style. This weekend, dress well and carry a great book. Choose something you're really interested in. Choose a book that reveals something about who you are and what you dream about. Go to a local café—no excuses now, since we have a Starbucks on every other corner across America! Order something delicious and simply be. Now, perhaps no one will come and chat you up, but it's a beginning, and simply being out in the world and looking great will add to your sense of confidence. Next, try wearing something just a little bit sexy (subtlety is the key!) to your workplace. Wear some great lingerie underneath—no one will know about this except you, but you'll see how different it makes you feel.

Next, look around at your circle of friends. Could you arrange a party? Nothing formal. Just create an opportunity to see and be seen. This is the first step to meeting new men and perhaps discovering a fabulous man that has been right under your nose all along!

French Lessons

START MEETING MEN in your natural habitat—on the job, with groups of friends, at your local café, at dinner parties. Build your confidence and desirability by dressing like a woman who's already in love.

Look around at your circle of friends and see if there are any gentlemen you could be interested in getting to know better. Ask your friends to arrange a small party where you can see how you feel in the context of a group. At work, remember you're a woman and dress sensually; be friendly, but professional. Make it a point to go out to lunch with your colleagues.

If you're young (or even not so young) don't burn your bridges. End relationships in a civil manner. You may need that childhood sweetheart. Keep in touch. If older, re-connect with past lovers. Keep your eyes open, and know that every man is a potential lover and if not, every man offers you the possibility of building your sense of self-esteem and confidence!

CHAPTER FOUR

French Women "Seduce" Everyone They Meet

WHEN THE FRENCH SPEAK of *séduire* (to seduce), they are speaking of so much more than the process of getting someone into their bedrooms. Rather, for the French, being seductive is a way of living and negotiating their world. It includes intelligence, wit, and a generous dollop of charm.

Here's how one French man describes it:

> *"Séduire"* doesn't mean that the end point is to put someone in your bed (although it can). I think, if my English is good enough, that "to charm" is more appropriate, or at least closer to the French meaning.
>
> *Séduire*, it is to make someone like you or your ideas. So *"la séduction"* is a skill that you probably want to have when you are a Casanova, or a seller, or a guru, or an escrow, or a diplomat, or . . .

So, it's a skill that crosses all borders.

"La séduction" is a talent a French woman might culti-vate for purposes of lovemaking, yes, but she will also em-ploy her charms and seduction skills to negotiate through life—to make certain that she is buying the freshest leeks at the market, or to get that parking ticket reduced (yes, in France, these things are often negotiable), or to get her eyeglasses repaired without having to pay an extra fee.

France is a small country with a close-knit society liv-ing within a complex social system, fraught with a lot of complicated bureaucracy. Things do not move as quickly or easily as they often do in America and because of this, the French woman learns early on that if she wants to ac-complish anything, she must be discreet as well as charm-ing. She will chat with the man who owns the *boulangerie*, the waiter at the corner café, the yoga instructor, even with her coworkers. She will not simply walk into a megastore and wordlessly buy her discounted bottle of wine, but rather she will go to her neighborhood wine store, where she's known the owner for years, and she will engage him in a conversation about the latest Bordeaux from Médoc. Is it really as fine as everyone says? She will ask about his chil-dren. How is the young Bernard doing with his studies for the *baccalauréat?*

Not only does a well-developed sense of charm help a French woman negotiate her world, but it is *de rigueur* (absolutely necessary) when it comes to her love life. How so? Well, French women live for pleasure, as Mireille Guil-iano described in her wonderful book, *French Women Don't Get Fat.* French women don't live in an either/or world.

They don't believe in feast or famine when it comes to their food and they don't believe in it when it comes to love. And so, our French women told us how they are just a little bit sexy all the time. Surely they are subtle, but they never forget that they are female and they have an undeniable power. And so they will *séduire* all the time, so naturally, so discreetly, that one may not even know one has just been seduced. The French have a way of giving a meaningful/meaningless sideways glance. When we asked Julie, who lives in the 5th arrondissement in Paris, how does she "seduce," she told us:

> I use my eyes! I seduce with a meaningful look. This is my key!
>
> To get a man back, I make him jealous.
>
> I am confident with my body, but I don't really know why. I like my body, I like to suggest its beauty, to make guys willing to learn more . . . And I love to dance, to feel my body, to shake it! The thing is that I always want to look pretty, because you never know what can happen!

Yes, it's just a look, and perhaps she might offer a little compliment, a small smile, followed by a subtle coolness. They will also ask for directions or a favor of little consequence, such as borrowing a pen. Perhaps they will ask for the name of a nearby restaurant, a wine recommendation. It engages the man and gets his attention, without giving her own intentions away. This way, they leave men wondering if they are the object of affection, or are they simply someone who is there to help the woman show off her charms in public? Perhaps she is simply using him as a ruse to make another man notice her or to build up her libido a little bit. French women are always practicing the art of seduction and refining their technique. Part of their practice involves taking their time, being discreet about their intentions, and engaging in some enjoyable chitchat that serves to inspire everyone's appetite for love and pleasure.

It's All About Pleasure

As Americans, we might say this form of seduction without serious intention sounds manipulative or inauthentic, but this is not the case at all. In France, witty repartee is a national pastime! It makes everyone feel a little bit sexy. Not only that, but it satisfies a certain need for attention, so that our French woman doesn't feel lonely or neglected to the point that she will "binge" on some less-than-desirable man, who is just a quick fix and ultimately leaves her feeling "hungry" and dissatisfied. We've all been there and done that— called up that ex-boyfriend in the middle of the night and when he suggests coming over for a booty call, we've said, *okay, why not?* because, well, it's just been so long since we've been paid attention to as a woman. We want to feel sexy.

Fast Food Lovers

And we do feel sexy, that is, until the next morning. In the unforgiving light of day, we realize, he is still the guy with the commitment problems, the one who can't pick up his own socks off the floor and will never remember to put down the toilet seat. And so, we kick him out and say never again and then we face our day with a lot of attitude. We snap at the man in the coffee shop. We frown at the guy in the elevator. We stomp into work wearing an armored business suit and we decide we hate men! That is, until the next time we are feeling lonely and unloved in the middle of the night.

This on/off way of living is not much fun. And certainly it's not pleasurable.

FINDING REAL PLEASURE means taking your time, and waiting for a lover of quality, and employing just a little elegant and artful subterfuge. Yes, we can often sleep with anyone we choose (sometimes within minutes of meeting!), but isn't it more delicious to wait until something really worthy comes along?

French women know this. They will chat up a guy, then retreat, then move forward a little more, then retreat again, all the while adding spice and intrigue to their seduction. They let a man they admire simmer for a while, standing by as the hunger builds to a delicious anticipation. And just imagine a French woman who has several admirers simmering on her stovetop, so to speak. This quiet build up toward pleasure is the key ingredient to how French women maintain their sense of confidence. And more than anything else, confidence is seductive.

When you are confident, there is no reason to give in all at once, or to even reveal all at once. When you are confident, you are mysterious and this combination is devastatingly seductive and irresistible.

French Women Never Look Like They're Trying Too Hard

Listen to how French women speak. Their voices are low and soft. They don't smile quite as much as we do. Their laughter is a little more contained. They're seldom boisterous or loud. They never get drunk. They don't act as if they know it all. Here's one French woman's advice to American women who are feeling that sense of battle fatigue:

> Don't be too sophisticated. Be more natural, more funny, more relaxed. Love of fashion and being sophisticated in clothing does not mean that YOU have to be sophisticated!!!!

There's a great deal of power to being natural.

Nothing is too obvious or appears to be orchestrated. This mystery and subtlety is highly erotic, because the French woman is always sending mixed signals. *I am available or perhaps I am not available.* And this is no game, because if you really consider how you feel, you know that you are not always sure about these things. You change your mind. That's a woman's prerogative.

Discreet, but Seductive

French mothers teach their daughters that they must be *séduisantes* (seductive and charming) as well as discreet from the time they are able to speak. This training serves them well in negotiating the sometimes treacherous waters of school and work, and also when it comes to finding a husband or partner.

America is a big country and we have the luxury of being able to move somewhere new and reinvent ourselves should we find ourselves "disgraced" in our hometown. We are not as close to our families and many of us live in anonymous cities where we can go for years without actually meeting our neighbors. We can meet a man on the Internet and then hop in our cars or SUVs and travel miles and miles for a rendezvous. If things don't work out, no problem. It's a big, wide country!

This is not the case in France. Very often, a French girl will marry a boy from her childhood hometown. And since the French family is the center of cultural life, both French men and French women are looking for a mate who can be discreet and will be able to negotiate the world with grace and ease and reflect well on the family. And while French women (and men) will have their secret liaisons, they generally don't talk about them.

In her fabulous book, *Entres Nous: A Woman's Guide to Finding Her Inner French Girl,* Debra Ollivier quotes Christophe, a French journalist with a seriously lush history of romance on both sides of the Atlantic:

> Everything in your [American] culture is defined like a contract, even the business of love. That's precisely the opposite in France. I've dated French women for months before I ever really knew who they were or what they wanted from me. After the first or second date, the American woman wants everything spelled out: "Are we dating? Are you my boyfriend or just a friend?" A French woman doesn't

do that. She doesn't give much away. She's comfortable letting things evolve naturally, but the ball's almost always in her court.

The ball is always in her court, because the French woman in question is probably not going on the traditional one-on-one date with Christophe, but rather she sees him with a group of friends. And by doing so, a man cannot really expect something from a woman, because he is not paying for an expensive dinner. This way, the pressure is off and a man and woman can simply get to know one another and develop a friendship. A seductive, heated, powerful friendship—until one day they fall into each other's arms and make mad, passionate love!

C'est Fantastique!

Doesn't this sound delicious? Wouldn't you like to feel a little more powerful and a lot more confident when it comes to your relationships with men? Wouldn't it be wonderful to know that the ball is always in your court? You don't have to be born in France or have a French *maman* to teach you these things. As an American woman, it is in your power to be just as seductive, just as charming as a French woman. It's simply a matter of rethinking what is sexy. Rather than "turning it on or off"—dressing in sweats for running errands and then changing into a miniscule cocktail dress with eight inch heels to go out at night—try dressing well all the time. Perhaps reveal a little flesh or wear one sexy accessory. Remember, less is more and subtlety is the key. Do everything in moderation. Think of love as a piece of really good dark chocolate. Don't go for the cheap stuff. Hold out for something fine and good and truly satisfying. Allow your hunger to build. Wait for the right moment. Savor it. Truly enjoy the indulgence, the sensuality.

Begin to "seduce" (French style) everyone. Practice the fine art of allurement. This is not about actually "catching" a man or forcing your husband to pay more attention to you. Be a French woman and treat every day, every moment of your life as an opportunity to feel the power of your desirability. Build your sense of self and tend to the health of your libido by dressing well, taking care of your body, and wearing good lingerie.

Use your eyes. Smile just a little. Do this whether you're seventeen or seventy-five. When you think like a French woman, there is no expiration date on love. Love and sex, desirability and beauty are not reserved for the young. Just look at Catherine Deneuve. Arielle Dombasle. Fanny Ardant. Juliette Binoche. Isabelle Huppert. Ségolène Royal.

Comme Vous Êtes Compliqué (You Are So Complicated)

Does all this sound a little complicated? Well, it is. But the truth is, you are complicated and love is complicated. French women know that this is a major part of any woman's charm—her unpredictability. While it was drummed out of us during the seventies when American women were trying to make headway in the professional arena, being moody and frequently changing our minds is still and always will be a female prerogative. French women never relinquished their right to be capricious. And it's time to reclaim this unfairly maligned feminine trait. Instead of thinking of it as a weakness brought on by hormonal fluctuations, consider our mood swings as great barometers of our mind, body, and heart.

And truthfully, men love the fact that we are different from them. French women have never forgotten this. Here's what one American man who lived in France for several years has to say about French women:

> I adore French women. When I lived in France as a twenty-five-year-old, my neck was perpetually sore from staring at all the pretty young things I'd see moment to moment on the street. Did I mention I hope to move back there someday soon? Their tall, slim builds, their stylishness—these things I admired, but also their tendency to live life a bit closer to the bone than Americans. Like their male counterparts, French women aren't as materialistic as American women, and on this basis alone are more beautiful in my eyes. Their beauty, to me at least, has an improvised quality to it. Spiritually, French women tend to be dreamier than American women, more prone to flights of fancy, more appreciative of passion, quirkier, more infused with *joie de vivre* and a determination to make the most of one's youth, more culturally informed. Also, I love the French language, the musicality of the intonations. A French woman can tell you to fuck off with such musicality that you'll thank her for it. Also, there is a formality to French language that can add a precious tension. My American friend once annoyed a pretty

young hostess in a nightclub. She responded, *"Mais monsieur, comme vous êtes compliqué."* In English this might be translated, "Dude, you're screwed up" or "Man are you hard to please." But, translated literally, this woman was calling my friend "complicated." Which he was. I love that.

Now, this may sound impossible to emulate. After all, we speak English, not French. But if you think about it, it is not all that impossible. We pay attention to our language and yes, rather than saying something like "you're screwed up," why not say, "well, you're complicated." It's a simple shift, a way of using English to create a more sensual effect. And truly, French girls don't have a monopoly on being authentic, being dreamy, or living close to the bone. It is true that we Americans may be more materialistic, but we are also joyful, passionate, authentic, and full of life. The problem is, we tend to reserve this part of our personalities for only certain occasions. Wouldn't we be better off expressing our joy or dreaminess and passion all the time? French women do. They know that while they are chatting with one man (perhaps the homely man or the old man or the man that we generally ignore), another man is noticing their seductive charms. Men all over the world thrive on competition, and it's human nature to desire what the other person has. The French woman indulges in every opportunity to show off her gifts. And this is the real secret to how she meets men.

French Lessons

GO OUT AND PRACTICE the art of seduction today. Ask for directions. You can smile just slightly, but use your eyes to communicate. Try this for three weeks and keep notes on what you've discovered. Record your triumphs. This will help you to build up a sense of confidence—one of the most important qualities to being a French woman.

Next, find pleasure from dressing well and being noticed by the world. Say no to the booty calls, the friends with benefits, the hopeless hookups.

And finally, allow yourself to change your mind. Listen to your intuition and embrace a deeper kind of logic that is your right as a woman.

CHAPTER FIVE

~

A French Woman Feels Good in Her Own Skin

IMAGINE WAKING UP in the morning, looking in the mirror, and feeling confident and beautiful. Imagine lovingly caring for your body with delicious soaps and fragrant creams. Imagine slowly dressing for the day, knowing without a shadow of a doubt that, yes, you are stunning in your own unique way.

French women start their days like this. Many of them will go to the day spa at least once a month for a facial. Or a French woman might make her own facial with ingredients found in her kitchen. She will gently scrub with a papaya exfoliating cream. She will take her time deciding on the perfect fragrance to wear for the current season. She will go to art fairs, and collect jewelry that is interesting and uniquely her style. And yes, she enjoys all the unique delights of being born female. She embraces and celebrates her inalienable rights as a woman. *How French!*

When We Burned Our Bras

In America, we fought hard for our equality. Our grandmothers and great-grandmothers marched on the streets in the 1920s and we marched (or our mothers marched) again in the 1960s and 1970s. We wanted a role in the world that had been traditionally conceived as a man's world. We fought hard for the right to take control of our destinies, to work at professions that were challenging and interesting, to pursue our dreams, to make a good living, and to question the stereotypes. It's understandable that during this struggle, we needed to give up many of the trappings that are considered "feminine." We wanted to be taken seriously and not be treated like a "sex object." And so, we adopted a bit of a masculine demeanor. If you recall the huge shoulder pads, popular in the 1980s, you know what I'm talking about.

Still, all through these times, there have been moments in fashion and beauty where the ultra-feminine look returns. Yes, we've had hooker chic and the custom of wearing our underwear as outerwear. However, in the professional world, we are still expected to emulate a fairly gender-neutral look, and it's getting really dreary. There's no reason why even the most serious of career women can't lighten up the traditional business suit with an interesting necklace or a colorful scarf and maybe some great heels.

The Either/Or Mentality

If we are only feminine when it comes to dates or sex, and suppress our desire to find beauty, to be beautiful and female elsewhere, we begin to feel a little confused. Our identity as a woman gets a little muddled and truthfully, this doesn't help our confidence level, because we are sub-consciously convincing ourselves that to be feminine is to be a sex object—only a persona that is revealed for the benefit of enticing a male.

But, why not be feminine just for ourselves? This is what French women have done for centuries.

The Wizard Knew

Here's the truth: French women are no more beautiful than we are. They just think they are. Remember the end of *The Wizard of Oz* when the Wizard tells the Scarecrow that there are great thinkers, philosophers, and brilliant men, and the only difference between them and the Scarecrow is this little thing called a diploma. A piece of paper. And when the Scarecrow is handed his piece of paper, his "diploma," he begins to think great thoughts too. It's just a matter of changing his concept of himself. A little psychological trick.

As simple as it sounds, it's the same paradigm when it comes to beauty. If you believe you are beautiful, you are beautiful. It's a simple switch in thinking, because once you believe you are beautiful, you take better care of your-self. You become more conscious, you dress better, you spend money on yourself. You feel worthy of all these at-tentions. You actually wear less makeup, because you can "see" yourself. It all begins with one small change. Perhaps emphasize those fabulous long lashes with some mascara. Add a little lip-gloss. Skip the blush and the blue eye shadow. Remember, moderation is the key.

The Natural Look

French women are famous for the natural look—wearing only a little foundation, a touch of mascara and lip-gloss. Some will adopt one artifice to emphasize a particularly beautiful attribute, such as false eyelashes or bright red lipstick. Still, less is more and the French woman will generally only emphasize one feature at a time. So, if she is wearing bright red lips, then she will leave everything else on her face alone. Or if she is wearing lots of eyeliner and mascara, then the lips remain neutral.

But the secret key to the French woman's beauty is actually not about anything she puts on her face or her skin. It's the fact that she is confident and happy with herself. Yes, it's true—beauty comes from within. You've always known this. French women *really* know this.

The one thing that makes you look and feel absolutely beautiful is your own unique self, your expression of heart and mind.

One French woman told us this:

> I think the most important part of a relationship is to keep your personality, to live your life and not your husband's life. You can love somebody, and love doing stuff with him, but you can't live for him, and he can't live for you. Your boyfriend loves you for what you are, so you have to keep this "what you are" forever . . .

By simply "being herself" the French woman creates a sense of mystery and intrigue. She does not succumb to the latest trend. And her sense of confidence also creates a little challenge for the man who wants to unravel her, figure her out, and make this woman his own. The French woman knows that her natural self is her most seductive self. This is because when we don't completely follow the crowd and buy into the latest trend, but rather do something a little different—we send out the signal that we are not so easily led. We tell the world that we think for ourselves and that we are confident enough to make our own beauty and fashion choices.

Here in America, we've succumbed to the idea that our natural selves are just not good enough and so we overdo the cosmetics, Botox our foreheads, and run to the plastic surgeons. But, in the end, do all these interventions really make us feel more beautiful? More secure? More sexy?

Reclaim Beauty

Here's what the writer Camille Paglia said in Salon.com on March 12, 2008, about our American movie stars at the recent Academy Awards:

> One could see it in the banal pack of glamazon young actresses on the red carpet at the Oscars—with their parched, stylist-honed outfits, their bony Pilates arms, their immobilized faces and simpering smirks, and their vapid, perky voices. All of them were upstaged in an instant by Marion Cotillard, the best actress winner whose French sensuality and sparkling vitality simply leapt off the TV screen. In France, there's still a mystique about female sexuality, a quiet magnetism that has been completely lost in

the U.S., where at least our major movie stars once had it.

In her landmark book, *The Beauty Myth*, Naomi Wolf says that "femininity is a code for femaleness plus whatever a society happens to be selling."

If "femininity" means female sexuality and loveliness, women never lost it and do not need to buy it back. Wherever we feel pleasure, all women have "good" bodies. We do not have to spend money and go hungry and struggle and study to become sensual; we always were. We need not believe we must somehow earn good erotic care; we always deserved it.

Femaleness and its sexuality are beautiful. Women have long secretly suspected as much. In that sexuality, women are physically beautiful already; superb; breathtaking.

French women have never forgotten this. While the women's movement came to France, it never created the kind of schism between men and women that we had here in America. When we interviewed French men and women, they all agreed that the "battle of the sexes" doesn't really exist in France. There is more of a sense of partnership. Oddly enough, we heard this expression: "*There is no cleavage between men and women in France.*" As an English speaker, the use of this word "cleavage" to describe a separation is amusing, but still it reveals how the French, even subconsciously, want nothing to get in the way of love and sex between men and women. There is no battle.

The Fear of "Disappearing"

Often, in America, especially as we get older, we start to feel as if we are beginning to fade away, back into the distance and out of the spotlight. And so we think we need more mascara, more lipstick. More. More. More, because we look in the mirror and feel this terrible sense of invisibility. We're living in a country that doesn't especially appreciate *la femme d'un certain âge*, or a woman who is not twenty-two, blond, preternaturally busty, with the body of a skinny fourteen-year-old.

Or perhaps this doesn't describe us at all. Perhaps we've become so discouraged by the media's constant bullying—shouting at us that we need to lose twenty pounds, get breast implants, revamp our wardrobe, Botox that forehead, and "surgically rejuvenate" our private parts—that we've given up. We've decided we'll be completely natural. We won't change a thing and we'll just let ourselves go. This wouldn't be so bad if it didn't mean not taking care of our bodies, cutting off most of our hair, going completely gray, and wearing nothing but sweats.

But this isn't living. And there is no joy there. And in the end, the media bullies have won and will continue to be the arbiters of taste and what is considered beautiful.

Take Back the Beauty

It's up to women to take back the idea of beauty, to show the advertisers and Hollywood and fashion magazines that we are here, we are beautiful, we come in all colors, ages, shapes, and sizes, and we're not going away. This is important. Our love lives are at stake. After all, are we going to let society determine whether we are viable candidates for love and romance? Are we going to accept the message that past a certain age, we should be thinking more about Metamucil and less about sex?

This is not the French way! In fact, according to a new six-hundred-page study of sexuality in France commissioned by a government agency, 90 percent of French women over the age of fifty remain sexually active. (This same study found that the average number of sexual partners for women between thirty and forty-nine years old is 5.1. For men, 12.9.) This would indicate that French women clearly go in for quality over quantity when it comes to their love lives and are able to keep their libido strong well into middle age.

You see *la femme d'un certain âge* all over France and you're particularly aware of her in Paris. She's the one wearing the fabulous boots, the mysterious dark glasses. Yes, she is slim, but she is also what Americans call "hot." Oh, and it's very likely she's wearing a short skirt with those boots. Or she might even be showing off a little cleavage. She could be sixty-something and she displays a confidence that is nothing less than inspiring. And in fact, her age simply adds to her beauty—there is a sense of fragility, perhaps, the wisdom of years, the sexiness of experience. A kind of worldly beauty that only many years of living and loving can etch into the contours of her face.

Equal Opportunity Beauty

And yes, French adolescents and twenty-somethings are beautiful too. Professional girls have style. Café workers have style and grace and attitude. Lots of attitude! But then, this is a part of the French secret. *Attitude.* We might mistake it for *arrogance,* but really, it's a form of confidence and it comes from knowing one's own worth.

In France, you will see tributes—statues, monuments, bill-boards, postage stamps—all trumpeting and heralding the breathtaking beauty of the female face and form. This has to help boost the French girl's sense of self-esteem.

French men tend to be more assertive and complimen-tary and flirtatious than American men. They don't worry about lawsuits quite so much and they know that French women appreciate being admired. This too conspires to help the French woman feel desirable. They get a lot of attention. Even if you balk at this, it's true. Every day. And while the French woman will dress well and take care of her physical beauty for herself and her own sense of well-being, she also arranges herself for the admiration of men. The French woman knows that once she leaves the house, all eyes will be on her. She will be admired, and indeed visually ravished. This is why she learns to walk with her head up high, with her shoulders straight. One French woman explains it this way:

> My preferred kind of attention, in general, is a
> complimenting look, or a simple *"Charmante!"* or
> *"Vous êtes charmante, mademoiselle!"* (You are
> charming, miss!) In the street, you constantly get
> some attention, especially if you are walking with
> your head up high, holding yourself up (like a
> ballet dancer), feeling feminine, others feel it too,
> and you look more beautiful that way.

French women learn at a young age that these attentions are generally harmless and they join in on the male-female mutual admiration society. Still, because a French woman will get a lot of attention on the street, she is careful about what she chooses to wear. She dresses well, even sexy, but she won't overdo it. She chooses one part of her body to show off—perhaps her legs. So, she'll wear a short skirt and boots, paired with an oversized sweater. Or she'll show a little cleavage, but wear a long skirt. She wants to get attention, but the right kind of attention.

And as shocking as this might sound to Americans, French women like to please men. But here's the good news— *French men like to please women too!*

Doesn't sound so bad, after all, does it?

What to Do About Our American Men

Well, here's our dilemma. We can celebrate our femaleness, our own unique beauty, and we can strut our stuff, but suppose our men just aren't on the same page as us? Suppose they've been taught to keep their compliments to themselves?

Many of us do dress to please men. We smile, we make eye contact, and we use our feminine wiles and still American men politely ignore us. Many American women talk about how, these days, a man will not open the door for us, even when we're carrying a bunch of bags and clearly need some help!

Or perhaps we do get attention, but it's the wrong kind and it's from men we'd rather not get attention from. And the nice guys don't want to be thought of as part of that group and so they've just stopped complimenting us, because they believe this is not what we want. Perhaps this is why American women are in such a state of despair. It seems, in training our men to be less sexist, we've drummed the masculine instinct to pursue right out of them.

But, the fact is that men still do (and always will) want to please us. If you talk to a lot of American men, you'll find they believe we want to be the ones to approach them. We don't want them to say anything personal about our appearance. We want to be the ones to ask them out. We want to initiate sex—when, where, how. And we basically want to take the reins of the relationship. Men are just doing what we requested.

Now, perhaps this was necessary forty years ago when we were struggling for basic equality and trying to get our men to be a little more sensitive, but now we've established a pattern where we do all the pursuing, while they allow themselves to be pursued. Obviously some kind of *market correction* is necessary. So, how do we subtly shift things to make our love lives sexy, fun, and yes—more French!? It's actually very simple. In fact, it's child's play!

Je te suis. Tu me fuis. Je te fuis. Tu me suis.

I follow you. You flee from me.

I flee from you. You follow me.

Imagine this scene. We see French schoolchildren chasing each other. First the girl runs away and the boy chases her. Once he catches her, the tables turn and he runs away. And so she chases him.

That's where we are now in America. During the sexual

revolution of the 1960s, we told the boys that we didn't want them chasing us. We told them that we want sex—lots of sex—just as much as they did, and that we too could separate our feelings from sex! Such bravado!

But now, the boys are running away and letting us do the chasing. We've been chasing them for over thirty years. And it's been really fabulous for them. They don't really have to do anything, except stop once in a while, pretend they got "caught," and then quickly run away again once things seem to become serious.

So, what can we as American women do? Well, how about if we "just stop." We're not going to actually run away, not yet. But, we're going to stop chasing them and just be. Be what? Be smart. Be sexy. Be confident. We're going to run just far enough away so that they can still "see" us.

Find inspiration from the French woman. When she doesn't have a date, you will not find her hiding in her house, crying in front of the Lifetime Channel, with a huge bag of Doritos. No, she is out in public. She is walking, going to the films, cafés, meeting up with her friends for an interesting evening out. Or she is simply going for a walk with a friend. She is not chasing anyone. She will not be found DWI (dialing while intoxicated). But she is being seen from a distance. She knows that if she is confident and stands her ground, she will soon find herself being chased.

Here in America, it may take a little time, but our men are pretty darn smart. They'll catch on and take notice before you know it. They'll see that there are women out there—gorgeous women, but they're just not chasing them anymore. Slowly, it will dawn on our men that we're not calling them up in the middle of the night. We're not arranging fabulous dates to get their attention. We're not willing to accept the occasional booty call. The key is to *show* our men that the tide has turned and not to simply tell them. Whenever you are dealing with men, don't forget, actions speak louder than words.

Before you know it, they'll take the cue and start pursuing us.

The truth is, just as we love men, they love us. They'll do anything we want. We just have to show them what we want.

Feeling Good in Your Own Skin

The French have an expression for this: *Être bien dans sa peau.* Literally, it means to feel good in your own skin. But still, this doesn't quite fully express the concept of *être bien dans sa peau.* This expression encompasses the unique way a woman presents herself to the world. She holds an image of herself, a persona, if you will. This image, this self-knowledge, is revealed in everything she does—in the way she speaks, her gestures, her clothes (she buys fewer than us, better quality, and only things that look really good on her), in her wardrobe, her accessories, and especially in her posture. Many French girls receive dance lessons, not because they harbor the dream of becoming professional dancers, but because these lessons teach the young French girl good posture and decorum and a kind of physical dignity that can last a lifetime.

Here's what one French woman said about the importance of holding up one's head and keeping one's shoulders straight:

> Some mothers insist on that when you grow up,
> some don't; taking a little bit of ballet dance
> classes as a kid helps, even some learning a music
> instrument, like piano, where posture matters as
> well; rather than soccer! But it's nice to see that
> U.S. kids are more active, taking soccer and all, it's
> just much less feminine.

Balance = Happiness = Beauty

The French woman strives for a balance. She knows that if she is happy with her love life, happy with her work, happy with her home life, and happy with her self, she will look and feel good in her own skin. She knows that this delicate balance involves taking good care of herself. She doesn't think of going for beauty treatments as indulgences, but rather necessities. And it's not about spending a lot of money.

She knows that her physical, mental, emotional, and sexual well-being are all interconnected and must all be treated with equal care and equal attention. French women know that when they feel good about themselves, they are confident. When they are confident, the world takes notice and answers back with admiration and so they feel even more confident, and so on and so on.

It's true about confidence. When we interviewed men and women, American and French—asking what makes French women so amazing—the answer that came up more than any other was their sense of confidence and self-knowledge. Here's what's so wonderful about this—French women don't have the market cornered on confidence. It's there for the taking. And it's time American women grabbed hold of some.

Less Is More

Start by buying yourself something lovely. It doesn't have to be a major purchase. Just buy a new scarf. An inexpensive piece of interesting jewelry. Get yourself a manicure. Wear just a little less makeup (or a little more, if you're doing absolutely nothing right now). Buy one cream. I recommend the one from L'Occitane en Provence. Take ten more minutes for your bathing time/after bathing/shower time. And as corny as it sounds, stand before the mirror and say, "I'm beautiful" because, you know what? You are. And if I were your French *maman*, I would tell you so—no matter what your particular look may be. Forget about some idealized version of beauty. If you don't have Angelina Jolie's full lips or Jennifer Aniston's hair—it doesn't really matter. Oh, and while we're talking about celebrities, turn off *Entertainment Tonight* and don't watch it for a few months. French women don't follow celebrities the way we do, and it's probably better for your mental health not to be assaulted by these discouraging images of "perfect" women leading their "perfect" lives—until they fall from grace, that is.

Jolie-laide

This is the French word for a woman who is not traditionally beautiful. Literally translated, it means "pretty/homely," but the word means so much more than this. It means interesting and beautiful in a nontraditional way.

What an amazing dichotomy. *Jolie-laide*. Yes, one can be both in France! Perhaps it's because the country and culture is so much more mature than America, and the sensibilities are more refined, or at least more complex. The French understand that with the complicated patina of age and experience and unusual facial features—a large nose or a very strong chin, eyes that are slightly off-center, lips that are devastatingly thin—a woman can be quite captivating. Not pretty. Not ugly. But beautiful.

For the French, beauty is not about the obvious, but rather beauty is seen as a kind of radiance that comes from having lived an intellectual and emotional life. The French cultivate the beauty of originality and artfulness. This takes time, because this kind of beauty cannot be found in a jar or a tube of lipstick (although these can help).

Still, French women know that they are most attractive when they are engaged and involved in their lives and their work. They are beautiful when they aren't even thinking about their looks, but perhaps passionately arguing about the latest Michel Houellebecq novel or the secret to cooking the perfect *blanquette de veau*.

A Few of Your Favorite Things

Something happens when you begin your day by taking a luxurious bath and pampering yourself with a fragrant body lotion such as Le Couvent des Minimes Honey and Shea Body Balm or any of the wonderful products from L'Occitane en Provence. French women take their time with the morning ritual. They may not indulge in a long bath on a workday morning, but they will certainly have a cache of secret creams and lotions for smoothing the skin, eliminating cellulite, firming their breasts and buttocks. One French woman told us that she rinses with icy cold water at the end of her shower every morning because "it firms the breasts." Do these rituals really work? Maybe. Maybe not. But think about what the fragrant ceremony of applying these delightful crèmes does for our psychological state. We become newly acquainted with our own body. We take time to care for ourselves. We rediscover our uniqueness and the wonder that is our physical form. This is the first step to self-love.

Scent and Sensibility

French women love to wear fragrance, because not only does their scent serve as an understated way to draw a man's attention to them, but also they love the way it makes them feel. In 1948 Fracas (which means chaos in French) was created by the French couturier Robert Piquet. Since then it's remained one of the most adored and yet exclusive fragrances ever produced. A heady mix of tuberose, orange blossom, gardenia and jasmine, it's the fragrance of choice for Madonna, Iman, Sofia Coppola, the designer Anna Sui and even Martha Stewart. Each of these women has claimed it as their signature perfume. You might wonder how one fragrance can have such an impact on a woman's life, but French women know that smell is one of the most primal senses and has the capacity to mesmerize and captivate.

The Power of Good Lingerie

Now, with all this bathing and pampering, the French woman cannot throw on a pair of old cotton granny panties. She wears great lingerie. Princesse tam•tam. Aubade. Dim. La Perla. Some French women will wear garters and stockings to surprise their lovers or husbands. Oh, and the panties always match the bra. Another French secret! They felt that they had dressed thoughtfully beginning with their most intimate garments.

Next, the French woman might put on a little satiny camisole. Her legs are waxed or freshly shaven, but if her lover likes underarm hair or finds pubic hair sexy, she will leave it natural to please him. Yes, to please him. Nothing wrong with that. Don't we want to please our lovers? Don't we want them to please us?

How Conceited!? (Not at All)

Honestly, to our American/Puritanical ears this might all sound a little self-centered. I remember visiting my aunt (not on the French side) and she found me holding my three-month-old daughter up to the mirror and pointing at her reflection, saying "That's you! There you are! That's you!" My aunt looked at me disapprovingly and announced that I was teaching my daughter to be vain and that nothing good could come of the habit of looking at oneself in the mirror. I remember laughing, because I had always loved looking in the mirror. My French grandmother had taught me to do this. When I asked the French women about this, they said, *"Of course we look in mirrors! All the time!"*

I believe a mirror can be a wonderful thing, when used with love and respect and a certain self-knowledge. It's a powerful tool, because it helps you see yourself as the world sees you and helps you judge yourself without emotion, but with honesty. Because, yes, it's true in many instances, we see something different from what the mirror is telling us, but I do believe we can use the mirror to begin to love ourselves. This is what French women do all the time. This is probably why they would never dare go outside without looking good. And certainly the French live in a visual culture.

French Lessons

LOOK IN THE MIRROR. Ask yourself, what is your best feature? Your eyes? Your cheekbones? Your bosom? Your legs? Now, find a way to accent this beloved part of yourself. Could you wear a bright blue scarf? Reveal a little décolleté? Add a little mascara? Wear a pair of textured stockings? Perhaps you might add a fragrance, or change a fragrance? Create a signature look that is yours and yours alone.

Next, create a list of all your unique and intriguing qualities. This can include your devastating smile, your thick eyelashes, your curvy bottom. It can also include your knowledge of Russian or your gift for the absurd. Now, make a list of your so-called "flaws," such as your ultra-fine hair or your slightly crooked nose or your practically flat chest. Reconsider these flaws. Accept them and relax a little. These flaws may not make you pretty, but they could actually make you truly beautiful if you learn how to accent them in a way that says you love yourself for being unique.

Find other ways to show that you are proud of being a little quirky and outside the cookie-cutter mold. Dare to be different. Dare to be confident.

CHAPTER SIX

Beauty and Brains

FRENCH WOMEN ARE WELL EDUCATED. School is very intense with little time for extra-curricular activities. Children are expected to declare a career trajectory by the time they're fifteen or sixteen. Around this age, a French child must choose a major in high school or technical school, either literature which includes two foreign languages (all students must start learning a foreign language in the sixth grade, and keep it up until twelfth grade, a mandatory second foreign language is started in eighth grade), or the sciences with a focus on either math, physics, or biology, or on economics or technical sciences such as arts and cinema.

All this at age fifteen! Around age twelve, the discussion on what a child will choose as a major begins and the pressure is on. True, many of the French find this system difficult and too rigid, because after all, one absolutely cannot shop around. In addition to the two foreign languages, most French students must also pick whether they will learn Latin and/or Greek, or not.

Very different from the curriculum in the United States. *Non?*

Clearly, this is a culture that values education and intelligence. And when we speak of education, it's not just about school and university, but a commitment to life-long learning. What does this have to do with American culture and our dating rituals? Well, if we begin by dating less and we meet our boyfriends, lovers, husbands, and partners at social events, such as dinner parties, we are going to need a way to capture a man's attention. Because, truthfully, there is some advantage to our system of the one-on-one date. After all, in the context of a dinner date at a restaurant, we do have a captive audience and so even if we are not particularly charming, the man has to stay put, at least for the duration of the date.

In the context of a dinner party or any mixed-gender get-together, we must be more like the French woman and find a way to capture a man's attention by lively conversation, an intriguing look, stylish clothes that are uniquely ours, an interesting personality, a gift for flirting, and yes, intelligence. Lots of intelligence.

Get Smart

If the American pastime is talk of sports, the French pastime is talk of good books, interesting films, and politics. The latest show at the *Beaubourg*? Just ask any French person and they'll tell you and give you a detailed opinion. Ask them about the latest foreign art film at the local independent cinema (French cinemas offer annual member-ship that allows them to see as many movies as they like for a flat monthly fee) and not only will they have seen the film and formed an original opinion, but they'll be able to quote what some obscure film journal has to say about the story. And of course, your French friend has also read the book. One French woman we interviewed said this:

> The French will argue or "debate" about anything, if they disagree. They debate a lot about new governmental laws, politicians, U.S. political candidates, the latest news, global warming, everything.

Does this mean that French women aren't sexy?
Of course not.

The French believe that being smart *is* sexy. They don't hide their brains the way we often do in America. The French just don't fall for the "dumb blonde" thing. Their blondes—Catherine Deneuve, for instance—are both brainy and beau-tiful. In her very funny and insightful book, "All You Need to be Impossibly French," Helena Frith Powell says "French women see intellectual rigour almost as important as their beauty regime. It is not enough to look seductive; you have to be cultured as well."

Men may be temporarily intoxicated by the cute flirta-tions, the awkward *"Okay, like, I think he's totally awe-some!"* kind of gal, but the truth is, this kind of girl gets boring quickly, no matter how pretty she may be. Brains last. Beauty fades. Let me correct that—actually, beauty alone will fade. But brains keep you beautiful, no matter how old you get. Again, look at Catherine Deneuve, born in 1943.

Difficult vs. Fascinating

We spoke to a French woman, who has lived in both America and France and has been involved with both American men and French men, about this habit of getting into heated discussions on art, culture, or politics, and how no one takes disagreements personally. She told us that in America she found that women who argued might be called "difficult" but in France, women who engage in such conversations are considered brilliant and fascinating. Does that mean as Americans we should stop getting into heated discussions on the things we are passionate about? *Absolument pas!* (Absolutely not!) But, do consider what kind of heated discussions you might engage in. For instance, if this argument is really a subterfuge for criticizing or diminishing the man you are interested in, and if it gets personal, then you are being difficult and, well, petty. The key to French women and the art of intelligent conversation is that it is never really personal. Thanks to the continuing influence of the philosopher Descartes, the French have a unique ability to separate from their emotions because they believe that since emotions come from inside a person, they can be tamed and controlled, so that they do not cloud one's intellect. On the other hand, Descartes believed there was such a thing as *la passion,* which is caused by an external event—a person or an object—and which is not controllable. This ingenious parsing of feelings is another indication of how the French are able to intellectualize love when it suits them. Perhaps this is why the idea of the mistress and the lover is a little more tolerated in France

than in America (but more on that later). Still, this Cartesian thought process allows for very cerebral individuals to
give themselves over to the tumult of a mad, passionate
love affair.

French Women Even Look Smart

In France, there are so many women wearing eyeglasses!
You would think there was a terrible shortage on contact
lenses. But no. French women like to wear eyeglasses. It
makes them look smart, but it also makes them look interesting. And yes, mysterious. You know that whole librar-
ian thing—well, French women know that there's nothing
quite as enchanting as a woman who appears to be a bit
of a challenge. Her hair is up in a chignon, she wears a thick
silk scarf wrapped around her neck and very trendy eyeglasses (that she may have spent months searching for until
she found the perfect pair). She knows that the intellectual
look adds to her mystique. A man will long to find out what's
beyond that brainy exterior. What does she look like without her eyeglasses, with her hair down around her shoulders,
possibly in bed after a night of abandon.

French women understand that romance and seduction
take time. Love is a ritual and to be appreciated slowly, just
the way good food is appreciated. Looking and truly being
intellectual simply adds to the wonderful journey from first
flirtation to consummation and beyond.

There is an expression in French: *avoir du chien*. Literally
translated, it means to have a strong character, but it also
implies being brainy and sexy and even a little foxy.

Be Complicated

In America, we have this either/or problem. Either we're smart and plain or beautiful and dumb. Either we're sexy, happening, hot-to-trot babes out on the town looking for love—or we're over-the-hill, old-maid librarians who are staying home with a good book and our three Abyssian cats. We have lost the art of the slow reveal and we've trained our men to think that if a woman is available, she will be wearing a red neon sign (metaphorically speaking), and if she is not, she will dress as if she has completely let herself go, and had given up on the notion of being beautiful, retiring to the life of the mind.

French women know that we need both—the life of the mind and the life of the body.

French women know that they are most beautiful when they are using their intellect. They'll not only read their local news, but they keep up on international news. They attend art gallery openings, read obscure literary journals. They'll meet up with friends and strike up a heated and passionate discussion on the arts, culture, and politics. They're full of opinions and they express themselves with verbal pyrotechnics. It's all part of the game.

French women don't join book clubs with just other women. They seek out social events that involve both men and women. The expression *"vive la différence"* truly expresses the French sensibility and how they love to be in mixed groups. Men and women, adults and children, old and young, urban and country. The French thrive on the essential differences between men and women, and yes, they can get into little tiffs about what men want and what women want, but the truth is this is all part of their flirtation. These arguments are often a subterfuge to fuel a little fire in the context of discussing the literary merits of the latest winner of the *Prix Goncourt* or the new book by Amélie Nothomb or Daniel Pennac. Or even why it's not worth seeing the latest Olivier Assayas film.

French women know that there's nothing sexier than revealing their passion in an intellectual arena, because it's the perfect cover for revealing a certain intimacy in the safety of discussion. How deliciously frustrating—for the man— to watch a woman argue her point and even tear up as she tries to explain how reading Stendhal changed her life. And while a woman may not be ready to begin an affair, she has still captivated a man, kept him intrigued by her expression of thought and feeling. He knows she has an interesting interior life, and that she is a deep thinker. He learns how her passions are ignited by certain philosophical and literary leanings. He knows what will move her emotionally. Perhaps he'll buy her a first edition of her favorite book. Perhaps he will find a poem that articulates her feelings and thoughts and experiences. By having this intellectual discussion, she is giving the man an opportunity to show that he is actually listening and paying attention to her. It gives him a chance to prove his worth. And she is giving herself time to decide if he is worthy. And in the meantime, there is no physical pressure. It is all about the life of the mind.

Earning Love the Old-Fashioned Way

Consider married life. It's true that sometimes during the beginning of a romance, sexual heat rules the day. The first flush of love is all powerful and there doesn't need to be a lot of discussion for the romance to succeed. Every night— indeed, every day—is spent in bed with only short respites to obtain food and drink and then it's back to the passion. However, one day physical passion is going to be balanced by life's ordinary demands. This is not to say that passion ever has to disappear completely, but even the most amorous couples will tell you that after years of togetherness, that wild heart-throbbing, rip-your-clothes-off-now sensibility must be backed up by intellectual passion, shared interests and desires, a connecting ethos, and yes, good old-fashioned companionship.

Remember the film *Last Tango in Paris*? A middle-aged American man, who speaks no French, meets up with a beautiful twenty-something French ingénue, who speaks no English. They meet in an empty apartment, and wordlessly and wildly they begin an affair that is primitive, instinctual, physical, emotional, and very, very erotic. In this hallucination of a film, they do not even exchange names. Nothing is revealed. And yet everything is revealed. And raw nonverbal sexuality is everything.

However, at the very end of *Last Tango in Paris*, the couple does reveal their names and histories. The sudden, horrible realization is that they have absolutely nothing in common and the girl runs from the man, screaming, *"Tu es fou!"* ("You are crazy!")

This is an extreme example, but it shows the danger of a love affair that is based solely on passion without intellectuality. There's nothing substantiating this kind of love affair. There's nothing to hold it up in the cruel light of day.

There's no shelter for the inevitable storm that eventually comes to even the strongest relationships.

Change. Change. Change.

French women are pragmatic. They're taught from an early age not to believe in the myth of forever. Often, the French woman can appear even cynical when she talks about love and marriage. She might act as if she doesn't really care one way or the other. But then, she will suddenly begin a wildly passionate affair and speak of it in grandiose terms that sound downright naive. It is this wonderful dichotomy that makes them so intriguing to men. American *and* French men.

But as American women, we too are full of dichotomies, complexities. We too often change our minds and turn around and do the exact opposite of what we said we might do. We constantly surprise—not only other people, but ourselves. Does this make us any less appealing? No. The world actually expects this of the female of the species, and actually finds our mercurial nature endearing and intriguing. However, in our efforts to make advances in the business and professional worlds, we've drummed this inconsistency out of our personalities. But why do so in our romantic lives? Why not be a little capricious, if this is our natural predilection anyway. Why not think of it as a wonderful gift and a unique way of thinking, rather than seeing it as a liability?

As a woman, it's your right to be emotional and volatile and then suddenly coldly logical and practical. Our gender has the unique ability to use our right and left brains simultaneously. Why not enjoy the perks? It would seem as if French women (for that matter, European women) are "allowed" to be much more emotional and passionate than their American sisters. Their men seem to accept their volatile nature as just part of being female. So, why can't we get our American men to be so tolerant? Well, we just have to retrain them. And the first step would be to give ourselves permission to be emotional and, when in the mood—coolly rational.

Lifelong Learning

French men look for a life partner who is intelligent because she will be cohost at all those dinner parties. Many of these parties will include professional relationships—coworkers and even the director of his company and her company. An intelligent woman makes a great dining companion because, yes, she is able to handle social situations with ease and grace; but more than this, she is a lively conversationalist and she is up on the news of the day. Youth and beauty may fade, but there is no expiration date on brains. And to be honest, don't we all want to ultimately spend our time with an intelligent companion?

Brainy Women Rock

We live in economically trying times. We all need to make a living and things are expensive. We all need to get a good education and be able to support ourselves. Life is too unpredictable to expect that a man is going to come to our rescue and pay our bills. Besides this, most men—even French men—appreciate a woman who is smart enough to be able to bring some resources to the partnership. As unromantic as this may sound, all men do think about this when they consider a permanent relationship. They all want an intelligent woman who has the potential to earn a good living and help support the family.

Knowing this, there's no reason to hide your smarts. French women certainly don't. French women know that their worldliness and intellectual curiosity keep men intrigued.

French women understand that men will begin to lose focus once they perceive that they *possess* a woman. This is because once he feels he "owns" her, he becomes a little bit bored. There's no longer a chase. Therefore, French women always remain a bit mysterious, even to their husbands. This might mean changing a routine, going to that new show, or even going away for the weekend with a friend or group of friends perhaps to attend a concert in the provinces. Yes, French women often take excursions without their husbands or boyfriends. They never "collapse" into a relationship, but remain, at the very least, spiritually independent. An intelligent woman knows how to shift the paradigm, shake things up, create an erotic mood by simply changing her hairstyle (or even wearing a wig), cooking an exotic dish, learning a foreign language. This subtle change is enough to alert her man that he has not quite figured her out, that she is still a mystery, and that if he is not careful and attentive, he could lose her to someone else more fascinating and focused. Be smart, like a French woman.

Read books. Go to films. Shake up your routine. Learn something new.

French Lessons

IF YOU WEAR CONTACTS, try wearing your eyeglasses for a week and see what happens. Go to an art gallery, but read up on it first. See that obscure film. Read a classic. Go to the cinema and see an interesting independent or foreign film. No Hollywood blockbusters (at least for a little while)! Read the reviews and get up to speed on the latest international news. Strike up a heated, passionate discussion on the arts, culture, or politics. Dare to be opinionated. Be smart and sexy.

CHAPTER SEVEN

French Women Take Care of Their Bodies

WHILE WANDERING AROUND BESANÇON, I stopped in a *parfumerie*. There are many of these shops throughout France. They sell perfumes, of course, but also health, beauty, and skin care products. And in fact, if you go to a *pharmacie,* you will also find pharmaceuticals and also a wide variety of perfumes, cosmetics, creams, and skin care products. Clearly, this is very important to French women, because *pharmacies* and *parfumeries* are all over the place.

In this particular *parfumerie,* I noticed a large advertisement that read, *"Strixaderm-MD Experts en Réparation."* I didn't really understand what it was supposed to mean. I did understand that Strixaderm was clearly a skin care company, somehow medical, and that the product "repaired" the skin. This much I gathered. But what really struck me was the visual. First, there was a very beautiful nude woman.

She was bigger than life—the size of a monument, sitting there quietly, completely still, while lots of little identical men in white lab coats, wearing eyeglasses, looking very scientific, were "working" on her body—repairing it, I suppose. The woman was so beautiful, like a goddess. Her skin was flawless. Her bare arms and shoulders, legs, buttocks, and hips took up the entire picture. The little men in the white lab coats were scattered about on scaffolding, gently "repairing" her skin. They were there to do her bidding, to make her beautiful.

The picture reminded me a little of the wonderful film from the Spanish director Pedro Almodovar, *Talk to Her.* There's a dream sequence in that film, a story about a man who starts off chubby, but then he falls in love with a woman and begins to lose weight. He's madly in love. However, after a while it's clear that he's actually shrinking—getting smaller and smaller. The power of love for this woman is making him waste away. By the end of the little story within a story, he is so small—a miniature man, in fact—that he enters his lover's vagina for one last time and disappears forever. It sounds like a Freudian nightmare, but in Almodovar's film, it is magical, heartbreaking, and actually very poignant. In effect, it dramatizes how the female body is awe-inspiring, incredibly powerful, and yes, maybe even dangerously so.

Girls with Superpowers

French women suffer from the same injustices that we do. There is sexual abuse and rape and harassment certainly, but the pervasive feeling as you travel around the country is genuine adoration and respect for the delicious power of the female form. Don't forget Joan of Arc, the 15th century saint and national heroine of France. Inspired by her unworldly visions—and while still a teenager—she catapulted the French army to victory.

French women are aware of their power and especially the power of their bodies. They are natural and comfortable in their skin and are taught from a young age *à prendre soin de soi* (to care for themselves). In fact, as young as age twelve, they will use creams and fragrant moisturizers after the bath. Their mothers teach them to enjoy their bodies and to care for them.

There is nothing shameful about loving and taking care of your own body. After all, it has to last a lifetime. A girl's *maman* or *grand-mère* instills the habit of caring for her skin and she will bring the attitude of self-care and attention into her adult life. In fact, as children, French girls will receive bath oils and bath salts as gifts.

A French woman loves her own body and appreciates all it does for her. She knows she must take care of it, just as she does with her mind. France is a Cartesian society and firmly believes in the power of a conscious, self-aware mind. While French women are passionate, they are also aware of the limits of the body. They think before they act. In her excellent book *French Women Don't Get Fat*, Mireille Guiliano talks about how much French women love food. They love good food, well prepared, truly fresh, and pleasurable. Part of the reason the French woman insists on good, fresh, pleasurable food is because she loves herself. She knows that she thrives on good food, in small portions. She believes in mind over matter.

We all struggle with the mind/matter problem. As American women, we might imagine it this way—we have a devil on one shoulder that says "Go ahead and eat that chocolate cake," and then an angel on the other shoulder who tells us, "No, just eat some carrot sticks." This internal battle leads us to severe dieting, which can then lead us to bingeing. Or perhaps we go from being a shopaholic and charging tons of unnecessary clothes to cutting up all our credit cards and not buying one new thing. This struggle is part of being female and all women experience it. But, our French woman seeks a balance. She will always indulge just a little bit, so that both her "devil" and her "angel" are appeased.

The Mind/Body Disconnect

In America, our Puritanism can get us into trouble. We are often disconnected from our bodies and this disconnection causes us to mistreat ourselves. And we mistreat our bodies not just with food, but with men.

Both French women and American women will occasionally bring men into their beds because they are a "quick fix." They satisfy our primal urges for closeness and comfort, and yes, sex. Orgasm. Release. During our interviews, we found that the major difference between American women and French women when it comes to "quick fix" sex was that American women tend to get more attached and fall in love more frequently.

One French woman told us:

I think when I want a long-term relationship, I

won't give to the man what he would want at the same moment. I think when I know I don't want a real relationship or it's just for one night . . . I will sleep with the man more quickly. Otherwise, I have to be desired, so the man has to be more patient with me because most of the time if he gets what he wants too quickly, afterwards he doesn't want anything more.

How pragmatic. And how French. So, she knows that if she wants a real relationship, she will make the man wait awhile and if she wants a quickie, she will indulge herself. But the distinction is she knows the difference between the two and doesn't try to turn a quickie into something more than that. In fact, this Frenchwoman told us, when she's had one of these adventures, she does not even exchange phone numbers.

Still, she seems mature enough to know that while the adventurous liaison might be satisfying in the moment, it is not ultimately truly long lasting or satisfying.

Taking Time

The ritual of caring for her body and her skin is simply a part of the French woman's routine.

French men don't complain about how much time a woman takes to care for her body. In fact, they expect this as part of the mysteries and delights of living with a woman. And the truth is, French women take less time with their hair than we do. They don't seem to go in for the hours of daily shampooing, blow-drying, and primping, but prefer to let their hair be more natural.

Still, as women, we all need to spend time on our bodies.

As an American woman with an American boyfriend or husband, you might think you will never be able to train your man to accept and understand your entitlement to taking plenty of time in the bathroom. How can you explain to him that the art of caring for your body is essential to your well-being? Perhaps the key is to show him that it's also essential to *his* well-being. Think about how far our men have come with enjoying and appreciating fine lingerie.

Back in the sixties, we raged against the Vietnam War, refused to trust anyone over thirty, and said we wanted to be completely *natural*. (Whatever that meant.) Actually, what it meant was that we would be nothing like our mothers' generation with the bouffant hairdos and the pouffy crinoline slips. We threw away our bras and let our hair grow . . . everywhere. However, by the eighties, we collectively got our MBAs and went to work. We wore power suits with shoulder pads, and at night at the disco, we wore our underwear as outerwear, with Madonna-inspired high heels paired with girlie ankle socks. By the nineties we embraced the culture of Victoria's Secret and decided a little artifice is a good thing.

But We've Always Been Sexy

Through it all, we were sexy. Yes, even when we wore those suits with the giant shoulder pads and looked like quarterbacks with law degrees. Men found us sexy. Basically, men love whatever we do as long as it makes us feel confident and beautiful, and as long as they know it will lead to happy women and great sex. So, if you embrace the French habit of taking a longer time with your bathing *and* it leads to more time in the bedroom, your American man will see the benefits and understand. It's true. We've talked to many men on the subject and the main difficulty our American men have with our taking so much time to bathe and dress and primp is that all this attention we pay to our faces and our bodies does not necessarily lead to our feeling happy and sexy and good about ourselves. But rather, we come out of the bedroom in tears, asking "Does this make me look fat?"

This is what happens when we buy into the culture of transformation through consumption. It's the American Cinderella myth rearing its ugly head. We believe that if we buy an expensive crème or start that get-thin-quick diet program, we will finally be happy. We will be sexy. And our men will love us. The problem is this ideal state of perfection is always out of reach. The world of consumerism wants it that way because then we'll buy more products, and we'll keep on searching and never give up.

And we'll never stop spending. In the meantime, the men in our lives are feeling neglected. Perhaps even annoyed. We've taught them that our caring for ourselves does not lead to more intimacy, confidence, or a sense of female power. It leads to less intimacy and more insecurity. And so they say *enough!* Or they will buy us lingerie for a special occasion and we will indulge them for the evening, desperately trying to block our feelings of inadequacy—drinking too much champagne and doing everything we can to ignore our excess flesh or tiny breasts or oh dear—that little bit of cellulite on our *derrières!* But you know what—men don't care about all that, especially a man who loves you. It's all in your head. This is why American men grow impatient with our fussing and focusing on our looks—because it doesn't lead to a better love life.

We have to rethink our beauty routines. Rather than using the bath as an opportunity to remonstrate over our flaws, why not do what French women do? Why not use your morning rituals as an opportunity for self-love and for building self-confidence? Buy some wonderfully fragrant after-bath lotion and really take your time. Get to know your own body. Look at yourself naked in the mirror and appreciate your own curves and lines. Do this for a few months, and your man will see the results—you will feel sexier, friskier, and more interested in the joys of the flesh.

French Lessons

START YOUR DAY with a luxurious hot shower, but if you have time, take a bath. Buy some fragrant soaps and definitely apply an after-bath lotion. Try taking a little less time with your hair and a little more time on your body and skin. Replace the negative self-talk with some self-love. Walk around the house naked whenever you can, and get to know and be comfortable in your own skin. Buy yourself some really sensual lingerie. And finally, pleasure yourself when you need to, or as the French women said, "There's no harm in making yourself feel good." And aspire to a love that's worth the wait.

CHAPTER EIGHT

The French Connection: Lingerie

The Power of Matching Lingerie

IT'S TRUE, we have Victoria's Secret here and we do wear sexy lingerie from time to time, especially for those romantic evenings, but our French sisters wear sexy lingerie every single day. In fact, every woman we interviewed emphasized the importance of good lingerie, but what was so surprising was their thoughts on *matching* bras and panties. Yes, they have to match, according to our French women. To do this, they will buy three pairs of panties for every bra they buy. When we told them that our bras and panties only match occasionally and usually that's just a coincidence, they shook their heads and wondered how we could do that? *It's like wearing a black shoe with a brown shoe!*

How can matching lingerie build a French woman's sense of self-esteem? Perhaps the copy from the website "Fédération Française de La Lingerie" can help us understand. They say they are designing lingerie (we translated the following) *"for hedonistic, demanding and free women, determined to be themselves but without abandoning seduction . . . lingerie that reconciles the body with the mind, reflecting inner beauty, an emotion that gives women elegance and a sense of well-being, making them radiant with beauty and naturally seductive."*

Yes, they are trying to sell a product, but could you imagine an American advertisement coming right out and saying that lingerie "reconciles the body with the mind"? Whether it's true or not, the very desire to do so is essentially French. And isn't it something we would like to do more of? Perhaps lingerie can help.

Do It for Yourself—Your Body—Your Mind

French women adore good lingerie. It is a delicious, secret luxury, not something they buy for their lover or husband alone, but it is something they also buy for themselves. Good lingerie makes them feel sexy and confident. Why save it for just special occasions? Actually, the French don't believe in this idea of saving our finer possessions for guests or special occasions. Just as the French will eat really good food every day, and not just when they're entertaining, French women wear beautiful lingerie every day.

The Travesty of Saving It for a Rainy Day

Have you ever done this? Bought a sexy black lace teddy and put it away, waiting for the day when you have a gentleman caller? But then, you get busy and you forget about the teddy sitting on the bottom of the drawer. By the time you remember it, you've already been involved with a man for three months and become used to hanging out in your pajamas and it would seem just plain odd if you suddenly put on the black lace teddy. He might actually think you're having an affair with another man. This is the problem with putting your beautiful things away for a rainy day. Whether it's lingerie or that silver tea service your grandmother gave you, you forget you even own it.

We get accustomed to only using the "everyday" things, and yes, our self-esteem plummets. We deserve to be surrounded by quality and beauty every day and it builds our confidence because the more we enjoy fine things, the more we begin to feel we deserve these things. And they make us feel wonderful.

Lingerie may not be visible from the outside, but when you are wearing beautiful undergarments, you know it. And somehow the rest of the world knows it too. But, the key is to wear it every day, so that you rediscover your own sensuality, just for yourself. No one is judging you. It can be your little secret. It's time to get out of the either/or mentality: wearing cotton Jockey's every day and then the Fredericks of Hollywood corset ensemble with the leather thigh-high boots and the bondage bracelets for those special occasions. No wonder we feel frantic and a little conflicted and not completely comfortable in our sexuality.

It's Not About the Bra—It's About the Woman in the Bra

The truth is, the lingerie in and of itself is not as important as the woman wearing it. Matching bras and panties, sexy stockings, silk camisoles—are really a means to an end. They are there to make you feel sexy and confident and comfortable in your own skin. Here's what one young French woman who now lives in America emailed us:

> Lingerie is important, but it's not all. Sometimes I don't wear a bra, this is really appreciated.
>
> In France, I would say that lingerie brands are different across women, depending on the age and also on your taste. I don't really like frilly underwear, so my brands are more Princesse tam•tam or Victoria's Secret.
>
> I sometimes wear a Wonderbra, but it's not the most important. I don't think that lingerie makes the difference. If the guy sees your lingerie, it means that he's already in your bed!
>
> So maybe no bra at all is a nice idea (if you can afford it!) . . .
>
> About good-looking, you can be sexy even if you don't have "the perfect black dress." When I want to be sexy, I show one part of my body, but not all at the same time (the stomach, the legs, the breast).

And now with the magic of online ordering, try some of these brands: Dim, Aubade, Princesse tam•tam, Barbara, La Perla, Kookai, and yes, Victoria's Secret. Oh, and the Dim brand sells fabulous stockings called "Dim Up" that stay up without garters, but with a little rubber lining that clings to the thighs—and they're completely comfortable. And they come in all colors. They're very popular in France because not only are they very sexy, they're practical. One

French woman living in the United States said this about
Dim stay-ups:

> I LOVED those. No problem with taking on and
> off for the bathroom, so sexy, make you feel like
> a sex kitten! French women definitely use those
> a lot! If they can afford it, they cost a little bit
> more than tights.

The Femme Fatale

In America, when we say "femme fatale," we immediately
picture Sharon Stone in *Basic Instinct*. Not so in France.
They have a long history of strong women and many
femmes fatales, such as Fanny Ardant, Emmanuelle Seigner,
and many others.

The French see the archetypical femme fatale as someone alluring and seductive. Yes, also dangerous. But, that's
what makes her all the more intriguing—she is a little
naughty and mysterious. She is irresistible to men and may
lure them into compromising positions, forcing them to fall
to their knees and do her bidding. In film noir and literature, she is the temptress, the enchantress, and even the
witch.

The modern French femme fatale can be seen in many
lingerie advertisements. She's often the one wearing the
black lace, the corset. Perhaps she is holding a little riding
crop in such a provocative manner, it makes men wince *un
petit peu* (a little bit). The French are very grown-up about
these things. There are subtle references to sadomasochism
and sexuality, but it is not treated in that *"Oooh, isn't that*

dirty?" little-kids-in-the-schoolyard tittering kind of way it is here. Rather, sexuality is respected for its power.

On my recent visit to the grand opening of a Galleries Lafayette in Lille, I was completely surprised by the lingerie department on the main level of the new store. There were several mannequins, dressed up in subtle S&M costumes, one with a riding crop, one wearing a mask on her face and chains on her wrists. Walking around I noticed a very tasteful display of sex toys in the corner. Yes, dildos in a department store! I will say this—they were very subtle and lovely looking, but still . . .

Make It Look Easy

French women never look like they're trying too hard. For example, a French woman will carefully choose one item that makes her look sexy and play down everything else. She might wear a sheer blouse with a pair of jeans. Or she might wear a leather skirt with a voluminous knit top. One French woman we interviewed explained it this way: *"The effect is highly intriguing, because a man can't be certain that you are dressing to seduce, or this is how you always dress. There is a mystery to this kind of dressing."*

A Gal Needs a Little Subterfuge

And why is this mystery important? Why is it important to always wear good lingerie and to always add a bit of intrigue and sensuality to your wardrobe? Well, it gives you a "cover." Why should a man know exactly what your true intentions are at any given moment? This is all part of the art of love. French women like to take their time when it comes to their seductions. So, while they might wear something that's a little sexy, it's just enough to get a man's attention on a subconscious level. He has no idea what your clothing really signifies. He can't know that you have any plans for him at all and so he will have to make an effort to get you to notice him. He will be intrigued when you enter the room. And he will be perhaps even a little peeved when other men notice you.

When you dress for romance every day, you begin the process of integrating your sensual self into your everyday self. You walk with a different gait—especially if you are wearing heels and certainly if you are wearing a pair of real shoes, as opposed to running shoes or flip-flops. Certainly, French women do wear Converse, but only if it's the latest style, in a particular color. It's a fashion statement. Otherwise, they stick to good shoes in black or brown with heels.

Try this experiment: ditch the sneakers for a few days and wear a pair of good shoes and a skirt. When you're going into town, park as far away as you can, and walk. This will be healthier for you, but it's also very healing, both psychically and physically, to your sense of connection to the earth, to being truly grounded. If you live in a driving culture, this is especially important. With all this driving we do, our feet never have a chance to completely and totally connect to the earth. And because of this, our bodies and our minds get a little disconnected. When you walk more, you also notice your world more. You appreciate your surroundings. You also realize how that shop down the street is really not that far away at all. It just seemed that way when you were driving because of the stop and go traffic.

It's Easy To Get Lost in Your Own Mind

Many of us work at the computer all day and we drive everywhere and our physical life is confined to the time we allot for exercise—either at a gym on a machine or at a specified time to run or walk. But, this is not truly the best way to connect the body, mind, and spirit. This is taking the body and metaphorically giving it a quick run on a leash in a fenced-in yard. This kind of physicality is disconnected from our intellectual and spiritual life. This body-mind disconnect can lead to all sorts of problems. We fill our bodies mindlessly because we never feel quite satisfied. Or we stop paying attention to what we're wearing out in the world, because we no longer "see" our bodies. Certainly, we don't have much fun wearing clothes if we're driving everywhere. Yes, we want to limit our carbon footprint, but consider another reason for walking—we get to be seen in our clothes. We find ourselves getting *the look*. And this inspires us to take care of our bodies and have fun with dressing up.

Why Driving Is Dangerous

If we drive everywhere, we lose the sense of our own flesh. We begin to see our exterior as metal and chrome. I noticed this when I lived in Los Angeles—the king of car cultures. I would watch women step out of recently detailed, brand-new shiny Porsches and BMWs and Range Rovers wearing little spandex outfits that honestly looked like under-wear. After a while, I realized that they spent so much time in their cars, behind tinted glass, that they really did see their cars as their "clothing" and that is why they didn't feel the need to wear good clothing once inside that chrome exterior.

Perhaps we exercise, but it is not pleasurable, because we are *driving* our bodies. We've got our iPods plugged into our ears and we are tuning out the people around us and even potential friends and lovers. And the workout ends up being something that verges on punishing. But, if we begin by walking and partake in the pleasures of seeing and being seen, we will discover the charms of the man who waits on us at our local post office. We will stop to sample that wonderful fragrance in the nearby gift shop. We will make it a habit to browse through our local independent bookstore. By doing this, we reconnect the body to the mind and spirit. And more than that, we ground ourselves with the planet. We begin to develop a sense of community, discovering common interests with the local shopkeepers, flirting with the handsome man at the stationery store, talking local politics with the gal at the consignment shop. So, being in the world leads to not simply making life better for us, it can make life a little bit better for the whole planet.

Every Day, You Inspire Someone

Whether you know it or not, every day you have the opportunity to inspire someone, to change someone's life for the better. Whether you know it or not, you are an example of how to be in this world. And, without even knowing it, you may be a mentor to a younger woman. So, if you don't want to look good for yourself, or even for your lover/husband/boyfriend, then look good for the next generation.

All the World's a Stage

Clothes do make the man (and the woman). And people do judge a book by its cover. Ultimately, your clothes signify how you perceive yourself in the world, perhaps in your profession, whether you're on your way to a casual meeting or a serious event. Hundreds of books have been written, deconstructing the meaning behind costume and clothing. Certainly, clothing has been used to indicate rank and social status. Costume is used in theater and film as a shorthand to indicate what role a character will play in the story.

Clothing is a form of fantasy. We have a visceral reaction to clothing. When we see an old-fashioned girdle with a garter holding up a sheer stocking, perhaps we have a sudden flash of our mother dressing in the morning, sitting before her vanity and straightening a stocking seam. We are six years old and we stand by the door, spying on her, in awe of this mysterious and very grown-up ritual. Or perhaps it's our father's tie collection. So many colors and fabrics. He never throws out a tie and so there is a line of them from thick to thin, from wool to silk. Some ties he wears all the time and some you've never seen him wear, ever. You wonder why. You wonder where did that tie with the miniature Scottie dogs on it come from. Was it a gift from a dog lover? Perhaps it was a gift from a woman he dated before he met your mother? Each tie is a little mystery. A little story.

You will never forget something your best friend in high school wore—that red plaid Catholic schoolgirl skirt with the giant safety pins all over it. Her dyed pink hair, and the pierced tongue.

Or maybe you still remember that day you visited your sister in college and she was wearing a vintage dress from the forties. She found it in a thrift store in Baltimore. It was a 1950s red silk sheath dress that made her look more like Elizabeth Taylor in *Cat on a Hot Tin Roof* than a college sophomore. You walked over to the luncheonette, Hon's, for coffee and pie, and she told you she had fallen in love with an architecture student and planned to wear the red dress to a party at the Copy Cat Building that Saturday night. And now, years later she is married to that architect and lives in San Francisco.

The Language of Clothes

French women understand the allure of clothes and the power the right ensemble has to inspire fantasies. With just the right combination of classic, simple looks and something very original—perhaps exotic or vintage—a French woman weaves a spell and gently nudges a man's subconscious mind, quietly promising him possibility, adventure, something foreign or forbidden.

Think about those fabulous lace-up ankle boots you own. You can insist—oh, they're just a pair of fun boots and yes, a little sexy, but on some level you know the effect they have on men. Fantasies of bondage surface. Or perhaps, he envisions you as an Edith Wharton heroine and this little ankle boot is something he glimpses under a long gabardine skirt as you come out of a horse-drawn carriage. You see, all clothing is full of deeper meaning and a multitude of literary and cultural references. French women know this and they know the power that clothing, jewelry, perfume, lingerie, and accessories have to evoke deeper, even nonverbal feelings. French women know that a red slip hiding underneath a simple black dress can have a devastating effect on a man. They know that the man doesn't even have to see the red slip. Just the fact that it is there will create an aura.

Men Are Psychic When It Comes to Our Underwear

Without even seeing it, they just know.

And now that you know this, your job is simple: be aware of it. When you choose what you will wear on a particular day or evening, keep it simple. Wear a pair of jeans or a basic black skirt, a white shirt, or a classic black dress. Now, look for that one addition that will create your fantasy. Men will begin dreaming of travel when you wear that Moroccan necklace you bought at the flea market. Wrap a sheer silk scarf around your waist and your man might begin daydreaming about harems. Or create the aura of film noir and wear those black patent leather boots with the sheer black stockings. A little S&M? Wear that sweater with buckles instead of buttons. A long strand of pearls can make you look like a cabaret singer. Wear a pair of dark glasses and a classic trench coat and suddenly you remind him of a secret agent.

Basically, you are simply using the power of theater and costume to create a mood. France is a theatrical culture. Subtlety is the key here, because if you allude to a fantasy, character, or era too literally, the game is up. Rather, it must be done with great care. The idea is to start with a very basic palette: good lingerie, simple (mostly solid colored) skirts, jeans, dresses, pants, and tops. Then, add accessories (sweaters, scarves, jewelry, jackets, belts, boots and shoes) that will create a focal point and reveal your individuality. The accessory you chose can become a part of your signature look, but know that once you have a "look," you can then mesmerize your man by suddenly changing it.

French Women Know That the Key to Mesmerizing a Man Is Change

One French friend Marie-Joëlle truly demonstrated the power of this. A beautiful woman, she told us how she changes her perfume according to the season. Just as in the summertime, she will make lighter meals—more vegetables, salads, cold soups—she will wear a lighter perfume too, when the weather gets warmer. Every day during our visit, we marveled at how she changed her look. One day she was wearing a luscious and incredibly romantic crushed velvet skirt in a jewel tone and the next day she looked fabulous—like a hip-hop artist—wearing big, bold, gold jewelry, great pants, and gold Converse sneakers. Yes, gold Converse. And, she pulled it off and looked amazing. Charming. Edgy and beautiful.

For this French woman, every day was an opportunity to play a role, to be different, to reinvent herself, so subtly that she kept her younger husband (and, indeed, I think all the men in her little town) on his toes!

This way of dressing for romance, of changing according to the seasons and our whims, is not just the province of the French. As American women, we know how to be theatrical. We know how to be sexy. We have learned how to dress for success so we can advance our careers. To be more like a French woman, then, we simply need to start dressing for romance whether we are at work or at home or simply going shopping—because life is romantic, if we want it to be.

Why not redefine the idea of dressing for success? Redefine what success means to a woman—taking care of your body and your mind. Wear clothes that make you feel not only successful, but also sensual.

French Lessons

DITCH THE COTTON granny panties and invest in some quality lingerie. Buy three pairs of panties for every bra. Make sure they match.

Wear high heels to the drugstore. Practice good posture—yes, even in heels.

Look at your closet and separate your basic classic clothes from your accessories. Categorize your accessories according to fantasies and pair up with simple basics to create a look that is just a little bit theatrical. Imagine you are not simply a woman, but you are "Woman!"

You make a difference. Just by being yourself, you are inspiring, and yes, even changing people's lives. You are a mentor and model. Dress for the part.

CHAPTER NINE

~

The Power of the Coterie

INSTEAD OF GOING OUT on the typical American-style date, imagine this: our French sister is invited to an art opening at Musée Maillol featuring her friend's latest work. There are several members of her coterie present—her old friend from her summer in Montpellier, the man from her office, her ex-boyfriend who she remains on excellent terms with, and then the older gent from her book club. The art opening is the perfect "cover" for our French woman. She wears a wonderfully put-together ensemble—her favorite little black dress, a vintage Hérmes scarf, and her sexy red pumps. She glides into the room, confident. She is not there to meet *l'homme de ses rêves* (the man of her dreams). *Mais non!* Rather, she is simply there to admire her friend's latest work. With that understood, she can flit about and chat with everyone.

In between, she is circulating, admiring the art, meeting new people, and practicing her feminine wiles. This event serves several purposes. First of all, our French woman is being seen as someone who is passionate about life and art. All the while, she is being noticed for her beauty, her lively conversation, her intellect. This art opening gives her an opportunity to dress up and look enticing—but without the sense that she's "after" someone or something. She is simply being herself. And by doing so, her male admirers continue to grow. This is because while she is chatting with one fellow in her cadre, there is another gentleman, someone perhaps she's never met—noticing her from across the room. He will have the opportunity to observe her in a group situation, talking, laughing, and enjoying life. There is nothing quite so intriguing as a woman who is involved in her world. Who is passionate and engaged in life.

Every gal needs a coterie. In America, we might call this our gang or our posse. More likely, our group of friends or our entourage. What is the purpose of all these friends and followers? They give us a social life. They make us feel great. They get us out in the world. They keep our calendars filled with opportunities to see and be seen. French women understand the importance of a coterie on an instinctual level. They know that if they are surrounded by a group of friends and male admirers, they will attract more friends and more male admirers. Men, in particular, are very competitive spirits and they want what other men have, and so if you simply appear to have the attentions of a few men, more will follow.

Another French woman, Isaure, told us about two sitcoms in France that she watched as a teenager. One was called *Hélène et les garçons* and the other *Le Miel et les Abeilles* (which translates as "The Honey and the Bees"). In this particular show, the "bees" were the boys who rotated around the honey, the girl. Both sitcoms revolved around the stories of a group of friends. The first group has Hélène as the main character, and her three or more friends who are male; the other has another girl or two, again with a group of male suitors. Isaure goes on to say how this seemed perfectly natural for her and that in fact she herself had a group of close friends who were boys. She called them *mes garçons*, because of the TV shows.

The notion of a coterie is so engrained in the French psyche that they don't even realize they have such a thing. However, when we asked about the reason why they very seldom have a one-on-one date and prefer to socialize in mixed groups, it became clear. French women know that they are most desirable when they are seen in the context of an evening out in a group. They can dress a little sexy, but no one man can think—*oh, she's doing that for me*. She is seen having fun, being happy, and flirting. Still, with her coterie at hand, no one man can be sure of his place in her heart. He has to wait and see, and yes, compete. This way, she can really see what kind of man he really is and whether he's in it for the long run, or he's going to give up quickly and pay attention to another girl in the group. Think about how much more powerful the French woman must feel when she is surrounded by possibility, men who are all vying for her, as opposed to the American woman who is dating one man at a time.

French Women Mix It Up

While our American sisters are going on a three-hour date with just one man or a "Girls Night Out" with only women, French women are mixing it up. French women know that there's a great deal of power in letting men see you in a group of men who are doing whatever they can to impress you. They know that men enjoy the chase or the *"you follow me, I flee. I flee, you follow me"* game.

We all know that when a man sees a woman surrounded by admiring men, he senses that he is missing something wonderful and that old competitive spirit rises within him. The overwhelming urge to wrest what the others have found pushes him forward. However, the very fact that she is surrounded by other men also forces him to slow down and get to know her as a friend first before he lays all his cards on the table, just in case she is spoken for and to make a move would mean confronting another man who feels a sense of proprietorship. Here's how a French woman explained the importance of her group or her coterie:

> There might be secret tensions there, between you
> and the boys in your close group of friends, for
> fun, cause we flirt and we are comfortable, and we
> know we are joking. Then, we meet new people,
> introduced by the friends inside the group, or
> randomly, and invite them to meet with our group
> of friends. I would not say that every man in our
> group is an admirer, they are just your buddies, and
> they do make you look good cause you have such
> a good connection, flirtation going on . . .

Friends First

French women very seldom become involved with a man that they don't really know. French women often meet men through their family and friends. Many meet early on in school or university. Later they will meet through social clubs, mutual interests, travel, at parties (lots of parties), art openings and film clubs, oh and yes, at their jobs. However, rather than immediately focusing in on the one man of her dreams, the French woman will take her time and get to know several men. She will not reveal her availability right away—married/single/divorced/with boyfriend/without boyfriend/with boyfriend, but relationship on the rocks, etc. Rather, she will subtly flirt—mostly with her eyes and a subtle smile—and see how the man responds. This is an important part of the process because everyone flirts in France—married, single, available, not available. It's a national pastime. Knowing this, the French do not rush forward, but circle around one another for quite a while. And this makes perfect sense.

Even here in America, oftentimes men are flirtatious with us, but the truth is they're not really available. Consider the man we meet at a party. He is flirting with us, laughing at all our jokes. He's so handsome and seems to find everything we say or do absolutely delightful. When we spill a little bit of our drink on the counter, he quickly fetches a cocktail napkin and cleans it up. He asks us about our childhood, our last boyfriend. He looks soulfully into our eyes and just when we are about to fall for him, he reveals, well, actually, he's married! And he's got three kids!

Is he a bad guy? No, not really. He happens to be there

at the party alone and he knows that he's going to get a lot more attention and have a lot more fun if he doesn't immediately announce his marital status. Knowing this, we need a way to get to know a man in the context of a group where we have the time and the space to find out more about his life, his personality, his likes and dislikes, and whether he is truly available or really compatible.

Build a Coterie

By building a coterie, the French woman creates a protective, yet ultimately porous, little fence around her heart. This way, the man who is truly interested in her must work a little harder to seduce her. But because there are other men (and women) around her—remember, she mostly goes out in groups—it's not so easy to see her alone. The man who wants to pursue the French woman is tested in a way. He must wait, he must make advances when there is an opportunity, he must be very patient, and yes, he must compete for her attentions. In order for the man to stand out from the members of her coterie, he might find out what book she is reading and read it himself, so that he can talk to her on a more personal level. He might find out more about a film she mentioned and invite her to see it with him. All this takes time, and fortitude. Clearly, a man who is not truly interested in our French woman—or only wants a quick romp—will not go to all this trouble.

And should he disappear (which is doubtful because the coterie is made up of both men and women friends who go out in groups), there is nothing lost, because there is still the coterie and the coterie can lift a woman's spirits, provide a social life, give her confidence, and build her sense of desirability.

The Art of Patience

To an American girl's ears, this idea of a coterie might seem cruel. *Suppose the boy really likes you? Why are you giving him a hard time? If you don't like him, let him go.* The truth is the French woman is helping every member of her coterie. She may not be interested in a man that is paying all this attention to her, but another female member of her coterie might find him enchanting. And by flirting lightly and by going out in a group, and being social, he too is being seen to great advantage. And clearly this other French woman surrounded by her own admiring coterie is being seen in a most flattering light. The French woman knows that it is much better to be seen in the context of a group having fun than in the context of the often dismal date between a man and a woman who hardly know each other.

When the Fling Is the Thing

French women have flings, just like we do. However, they seem to truly understand that a fling isn't going to lead to long-term romance. Here's how one French woman explained it:

> Of course, if you think that this is the one, you should wait before sleeping with him. When I sleep with a guy the first night, I know that it's just for

sex, and I enjoy it. This sex-relation can last, and sometimes can become a serious relationship, but it's very rare. So I can tell that I had two kinds of love affairs: just for sex (the guy is cute, you fit well in bed—so enjoy!—usually it doesn't last, better to change frequently, I get bored . . .), and long-term relationships, from six months to three years (in that case not only do you fit well in bed, but you also want to share things in life . . .).

So if you sleep with a guy you don't really know, usually it's just for sex, even if it lasts months.

If the guy doesn't call back, it's because it was just for sex!

The most important thing: be yourself! Don't do something you don't want and you will regret.

Yes, be yourself. So, if you can handle a fling and don't mind if the man doesn't call you after a night of hot sex, well then, that's okay. Still, it may not be okay further on down the road, so it's important to check in with your heart every now and then. Because, truthfully, this may be cool when we're younger, but as we get into our thirties and forties, we may not be quite so cool with sharing our bodies with strangers who don't call afterwards.

American Men Are Building a Coterie via the Internet

Many American men use the Internet as a kind of coterie-building system. They will "meet" hundreds of women and then narrow it down to a group of about forty with whom they will correspond. This group of women then becomes their cyber-coterie and the man can then get to know each individual woman by email and perhaps by phone calls. Oftentimes, men will take six months before even suggesting a meeting. This way, our American male has been able to "date" in cyberspace without spending money on dinners or movies. He's been able to create a kind of intimacy through writing. And finally, when he meets with a woman, he can then suggest they sleep together—after all, they've "known" each other for six months.

Here's the problem with cyber-coteries. The American woman is still "isolated." She doesn't "see" the other women he's cyber-dating and he doesn't "see" her many cyber-admirers. This sets up a false intimacy (and gives him the impression that he's the only man in her life and he has no competition). Once they meet in the flesh, there is no group, no real coterie, no real history, and nothing to slow things down and create a community. He doesn't see other men watching her or flirting with her and he doesn't have any idea that there may be others who admire her. She has so much less power than if she met him through a real coterie of male and female friends. Yes, Internet dating seems clever and efficient, but ultimately you still want to go out within the context of a coterie.

Take Your Time

The French woman knows that if she is seriously interested in a man, she will not sleep with him too quickly. She will only sleep with a guy right away if she sees no future in it. Yes, this sounds counterintuitive, but every single French woman we interviewed said something similar to this.

Strangers with Candy

Yes, the French woman does have *des petites aventures*, but she doesn't always talk about them the way American women do. Often, her adventure will become part of her *petit Jardin Secret* (more on the Secret Garden later) and she discreetly keeps this little tryst to herself. One French woman told us of a friend she has known for over ten years, who just revealed that she has been having an affair with a married man for over five years.

Still, even if our French woman does indulge in a "secret garden" affair, she will not drop out of circulation and leave behind her coterie.

Keep the Love Flowing

A French woman is pragmatic about her love affairs and knows that if the initial infatuation wears off, she will need her coterie to build up her confidence, to socialize with, to be seen, and to see who else is a possible candidate for her affection. And she can take her time when she's considering the possibility of a love affair with a member of her coterie. There's no reason to rush things, because she sees this man often in the context of a group. Isn't it delicious to let the attraction and sexual tension build over time? Doesn't this make the final consummation that much more pleasurable? And of course with food and wine and love and sex, for the French woman, it's all about pleasure and *passion*. And for the French woman, the longer she waits, the more serious and long-lasting the affair will be. She knows the difference between the adventure and the more substantial relationship. One can be an instant gratification. The other takes time.

A Coterie Lasts a Lifetime

Even after a French woman is married or she lives with her partner or boyfriend, she will continue to socialize with her coterie. They are her closest group of friends, after all. And of course, the tradition of the French dinner party makes all this possible. This keeps flirtation alive and well. Through new introductions, a French woman can add a new member to her coterie or renew an old alliance. These flirtations serve to keep the French woman's husband on alert—if he is not attentive, another man may capture her heart. Many French women will be sure to end things with their old boyfriends on good terms. This way, they can still be part of the coterie, and keep things a little spicy. True, after she's married, our French woman might not see her old boyfriends anymore, but certainly many do stay in touch. Here's what a French woman wrote to us about the role of former lovers:

> I would say yes, a lot of us will stay in touch with exes, except if it was a major relationship, a long-term boyfriend, and it ended very badly. If it was just a lover, the connection will still be there, even if there is no more sex with him. It's just an interesting sexual tension, a secret connection.

This is an essential part of your coterie. While you may not be even attracted to your ex-boyfriend, his very presence adds to your allure—so why permanently and completely throw him over? And besides, perhaps one day, he'll turn out to be the one. Or perhaps another man, feeling intrigued by the obvious connection, will make a move. The point is, with a coterie of friends, you are being seen whether you are "seeing" someone or not.

Where to Find Your Coterie

Your coterie is often already around you and you just don't realize it. These men and women could be old friends, new acquaintances, coworkers, friends of friends. Even ex-boyfriends or ex-husbands. French women know that one man begets another and another and that when she is seen as being in demand, other men will follow.

The key word here is "admirers." French women don't waste their time and energy getting intimate with a whole variety of men. The French woman knows that she wields her greatest power when she is still a mystery, still seemingly "unconquered." A French woman will flirt, but she always remains very discreet when it comes to her love life. This way, she is able to give the impression that she might one day be available if the circumstances are right. How does she do this? She never collapses into a relationship—staying inside, locking the door as if she is "done" and no longer needs to show herself off, even after she's married. Rather, she takes care to look her best and be intellectually and socially active. In other words, she gets around.

Some French women "keep" their lovers. It's a small country. If you're French, you're probably going to eventually run into your old lover, anyway. It's not like here in America, where you can just move to another state and avoid that old flame. In France, especially since it's a culture of interconnected social groups, it is not an easy thing to leave a lover and never see him again. Therefore, one must be civil and leave a relationship on good terms. You may be seeing someone else, you may be madly in love, or married or newly free, but this former lover will always have a soft spot in his heart for you. And if you do nothing at all, but greet him civilly, others in your coterie will feel the unspoken feelings, and the history.

How to Develop Your Own Coterie

Many American women claim that they can't create a coterie because they don't have any admirers. This is simply not true. We all have admirers. We might not realize it or we might say, *"Oh, that's just Bob, my old friend from college. He's not an admirer!"* But, imagine this—you invite him to join you and your friends at the watering hole on South Street and then the following week, you invite him to your best friend's dinner party. After that, you ask him if he wants to join you and your friends at that new art opening. While there, he runs into his friend from work— Michael. He introduces Michael to you and you know what—sparks fly. Michael joins your group, but he seems more interested in your friend Sheri. You flirt with Bob. It's light and nothing serious, but then Sheri gets a little jealous and she starts a fling with Bob. Michael has a new interest in you. Then, the man from your work happens to be at the art opening that night and sees all these men vying for your attention and he is completely smitten. And before you know it, you have formed a fabulous coterie!

French Lessons

CONSIDER HOW MANY MEN in your life admire you (and you admire) and make a list in a private notebook that no one but you will ever see. Now, consider how you might develop these "friendships" and guide them along so that you always have a gentleman who would love to meet you for dinner or accompany you to a concert or party. Even if you're married, it's important to have an escort occasionally. So, be sure to attend to your list by calling and chatting casually, sending a note of congratulations when they've achieved a milestone or simply sending a brief and friendly (personal, not group) email just to say hello.

Next, build a coterie of your own. Start by flirting (ever so lightly) with everyone. Make a list of three to seven men who admire you. Who are these men? Get to know them better. It might be drinks after work with someone at your office. Use the cover of business or a mutual interest to arrange a meeting. Be sure to remain completely platonic. Still, be friendly and interested in them, but not so much that they think you're "after" something. You are in fact after nothing more than building up your confidence and sense of desirability. And that's very French.

CHAPTER TEN

❧

French Women et le Jardin Secret
(The Secret Garden)

THROUGH THE CENTURIES, French women have learned that it is not always wise to wear their hearts on their sleeves. The French woman knows better than to reveal all too quickly and that sometimes it is better to simply wait and watch. If you look at the face of the French woman, you'll see that she's more self-contained, at least in public. Within a secure circle of friends, she may be much more effusive and emotional, but generally emotions are kept private. In fact, the French feel they need to be "controlled." You can thank Descartes.

Certainly, when it comes to love, there are those moments when a French woman may become emotional and confess her most heartfelt feelings, but more often than not, she will hold her cards close to her breast and maintain a mysterious air. Does this make the men in her life lose interest and run? *Au contraire!* She finds that this opaqueness only heats things up.

We live in a very different culture. We live in a great big sprawling and very young country. We're an expansive society. We laugh loudly. We express our emotions freely. Some of us eat big meals and drive big cars on big eight-lane freeways. We take up a lot of space, because we have (or we think we have) a lot of space. Many of us live in big houses and when we have guests over, we like to give them a tour of the entire house, including the private rooms—the bedrooms, the bathrooms. Not so with the French. They will seldom show you the rooms beyond the kitchen, dining room, and living room.

But we love to throw our doors open.

However, when it comes to our relationships, this expansiveness has not always served us. Yes, it's fun to go out with the girls and gossip about our latest conquests. It feels wonderful to cry freely and laugh loudly. And we stick by our culture of confession and the belief that if we are honest and communicate and reveal all, men will appreciate this and accept us for ourselves—love us for our generous hearts and forgive us our foibles.

Inside the Secret Garden

As Americans, we strive for complete honesty. However, this is not always in our best interest. French women know this. This is why they keep their *Jardin Secret* (Secret Garden). The Secret Garden can be her state of mind or a fantasy place she can visit when she daydreams. It could be a secret intellectual passion. Perhaps she loves to write poetry or she's addicted to romance novels. Her Secret Garden could be a hobby that no one in her usual circle knows about, such as playing chess. Or it could be a group of friends, such as those American girls she met during her year abroad, and her French friends don't know about them or that secret world she lived in. It could be a private relationship that's completely platonic, but with someone she doesn't bring into her group of friends, or even her coterie.

And finally, a French woman's Secret Garden might be a secret love affair. This love affair may be no more than a slightly dangerous flirtation, or it might be something more. She may be married and indulging in this or she may be single, but she does not want her coterie to know about this Secret Garden. Indeed, she might actually have a full-fledged lover. But she won't generally broadcast it; it is her secret.

Behind Closed Doors

And yes, the French do have affairs, just as Americans and men and women all over the world have affairs. The difference is the French woman does not discuss her affair as openly. And hopefully, if the person in question is a government official, they will not become fodder for the tabloids (although this is changing in France, as we speak).

In general, the French love their privacy more than Americans do. A French woman knows that her Secret Garden needs to be protected and kept secret if it is to remain a powerful part of her imaginary life. This is the other advantage to having a Secret Garden—it fuels one's fantasy life and creates a kind of internal world that nourishes and feeds one's psyche. When the outside world is exhausting and overwhelming, the French woman might retreat to her bedroom, draw the curtains and read a romance novel, or practice her yoga or simply lie down and think about Jean-Claude and that time they kissed on the ski lift in Chamonix. She might even call her old lover, François, and have a glass of wine and talk late into the night about the time they got caught in the rain on Mont-Saint-Michel and ended up spending the night in the little bed and breakfast that served the most decadent assortment of croissants and pastries, fresh squeezed orange juice, fresh yogurt, and fabulous coffee.

Even though the affair is long over, his voice on the telephone brings back all the memories, and even though she will probably never be intimate with François again, the attraction is always there. It's palpable. She can hear it in his voice, late into the night, as they whisper and reminisce about old times. This lover from her past is this French woman's secret, and by the time the late night conversation is over, and the two of them are falling asleep on the phone, miles apart, the world has grown warm and toasty and she is feeling a newly restored sense of allure, sensuality, and yes, confidence.

Where the French Woman Gets Her Confidence

This late night "visit" with her secret "lover" will stay with her during the next day and the day after that, and perhaps even for weeks to come. She will have a new lilt to

her step, and she will brim with a sense of her own desirability. This is wonderful for the French woman's self-
esteem. But more than this, men notice!

No, she doesn't have to say a word about her *Jardin
Secret*, and it doesn't necessarily have to involve a phone call
to an old lover—but rather something that she keeps private.
The very fact that she has a place to go that is hers and
hers alone adds a sense of mystery and intrigue to her. All
men (yes, American and French!) are attuned to a woman's
mood. They've learned it from childhood—when mama is
in a good mood, things go well, but when mama is un-
happy, well that's another story.

And so, a French woman's boyfriend can feel that she
is not obsessed with their relationship. She is not hanging
on every word he says. She is not so concerned about whether
he has given her a gift for Valentine's Day or called her
on Wednesday. In fact, the tables are turned, because he can
sense that she has other things (or yes, even other men) on
her mind. He knows that she is not completely his. She has
not abandoned her individuality to the relationship. She remains separate.

Even when they are together, he knows, she is spiritually free. And this is true even when they're married. The
French woman's *Jardin Secret* is a place she goes to spiritually, intellectually, and sensually to restore her sense of
independence and power.

She finds a special place or passion. Her Secret Garden
might just be a fascination with a book she found in the
library. She finds a café where she goes every afternoon
to read. She emerges an hour later, somehow changed by

this book. She returns to her day-to-day life with a new-found sense of who she is in the world separate from her lover/partner/husband/boyfriend. Then, when she returns to be with him or to go out to a dinner party—she will surprise everyone with a little comment about the ancient art of calligraphy on rice paper. Still, even when someone asks, incredulously, *"How did you know that?"* our French woman will smile mysteriously and say, *"I don't know . . . I just know."* She will not reveal all the details of the library she goes to and the café where she reads every day, and the delicious cup of tea she enjoys during her intellectual foray into her *Jardin Secret*.

And men have their secret gardens, as well. They like to go out and fish or be with their friends. There's nothing wrong with this, because it too makes them more interesting and intriguing. Individuality is the thing that will keep any relationship alive, because you are continually offering new things to one another and there are always surprises.

French Women Are Mysterious

The *Jardin Secret* is the wellspring of this sense of mystery. As American women, we may find the whole idea of remaining mysterious silly. Why shouldn't we be honest? Isn't that the best policy, after all? But, there is a difference between being honest and spilling out a lot of information that is best kept behind closed doors. Why tell everything? Does it help your relationship with your husband if he knows you're worried about your cellulite? Does your boyfriend really need to know that you bought a pair of shoes today that were fifty percent off? Do your friends really want to know how your bridge came out and you had to rush to the dentist to get it fixed?

It may not seem as if this is a big deal—it may seem like simple chitchat, when we reveal the minutia of our daily lives—but the truth is, this unnecessary information chips away at our sense of self. We get drained (and our friends and lovers feel drained) and after a few days of this, we begin to feel as if little pieces of our personality, our inner lives, have been scattered to the wind. This depletes us and leaves us feeling weakened, emotionally exhausted, and so we might do something that feels comforting in the moment, but is really self-destructive, such as a last minute hookup with an ex or a date with a carton of Ben and Jerry's Chunky Monkey.

What We Can Learn from Proust

The French woman does occasionally feel emotionally drained. We all do; we are human, after all. But, *le Jardin Secret* serves as a place of refuge for her. She truly "lives" in her body and so she knows when she needs to be replenished, and so her Secret Garden might just mean an opportunity to stay in bed all day and relax.

The French woman is not afraid to turn down an invitation (giving proper notice and explanation). She does not overextend herself socially and become a social butterfly, flitting from party to party, exhausting herself, drinking too much, talking too much. She knows that as Marcel Proust said, "An absence, the decline of a dinner invitation, an unintentional coldness, can accomplish more than all the cosmetics and beautiful dresses in the world."

And a word on drinking too much: French women seldom drink too much. French women do not become the party girl that everyone is secretly laughing at behind her back. A French woman knows that while men may enjoy the company of a wild and crazy girl and even have a fun time with her every now and then, men generally do not take this kind of woman seriously and if she indeed overindulges in food or drug or drink, it is doubtful that he will consider her as a candidate for a long-term relationship. The French do drink wine of course, and champagne, but it is generally with food, and always with company.

Keep Your Head

The French family, the schools, and the community teach their young ones the importance of keeping calm in the face of emotional turmoil. In fact, it is a point of French pride to keep cool, certainly rational, and never fall into an irrational tumult and *perdre la tête* (lose one's head). In fact, the general rule for drinking is to have one glass of water for every glass of wine.

We can again thank Descartes, for this philosophy of keeping one's emotions in check. French women don't even go to psychotherapists as much as we do, simply because they believe that their psychological struggles are private and that one must exert intellectual power and harness one's emotions so that they are kept in proper proportion. This takes discipline and a sense of moderation. If she does seek the help of a psychotherapist, she will keep it private. She might discuss her difficulties with her mother, but she will certainly not broadcast her latest misadventure or heart-break on the Girlfriend Network. This is not to say that French women do not get emotional and cry. Younger girls will talk to their friends about their boy troubles, while older ones wait until they really, really know their friends. Part of the reason behind the French woman's reticence to share information about their man (whether it's about how he's a great lover or how their relationship is on the rocks) stems from the jealousy factor and, as one French woman told us, *"the knowledge that another woman might steal your man."*

It is true that French women do not seem to trust one another the way American women do. However, I think we all know of someone who lost her man to a close friend. And so, perhaps the French woman's ability to be discreet is not such a bad thing. Does this sound cold? Does it sound impossible for the American woman to emulate? It's not, really. Once we begin to modulate our emotions, we begin to create a new pattern. And the Secret Garden can help.

There's No Such Thing as Perfection

French women do not believe in perfection. In earlier times, many marriages were arranged. While our American grand-mothers and mothers might have been courting and dat-ing and going out with several men for a number of years before deciding to marry, French women do not take a lot of time with this process and generally marry (or more likely in today's France—simply move in with) their partners early on. Many French women still only have one partner in an entire lifetime. This might sound archaic to an American girl, especially if you live in a city, and are under thirty. It's easy to get on that dating treadmill where we date a man for a few weeks, we see him practically every day. Things get very intense. We think this is it—this is true love. We sleep with him and spend every possible moment together. He's practically moved in by the time we've known each other a month. We've exchanged all our stories from childhood—how we had terribly crooked teeth as a kid and had to wear braces for years and how the other kids in school made fun of us and called us "metal mouth." We work ourselves into an emotional froth, describing the injustice of it all, the humiliation, as if it just happened the day before yesterday. We're in a terrible hurry to tell all right away. And he shares all his triumphs and tribulations and suddenly there's nothing left to tell. Nothing to discover.

This is not mysterious. This is not sexy. And it's definitely not French.

Of course, it's okay to reveal a childhood wound, but it's not necessary to relive the whole thing in vivid detail. French women do not treat their lovers as if they were their father confessors or therapists or *mothers*. French women understand that no one man can be all things to one woman. She is not nearly as idealistic about love and marriage as we are in America. She keeps her Secret Garden as a place where she can seek emotional solace. Or yes, perhaps she will keep a Secret Garden friend to whom she goes with her personal struggles.

We Are Family

As Americans living in such a big country, often removed from family and close friends, we lose our "anchor." And we begin to depend too much on our men. They are only men, after all. There are pragmatic reasons for not depending on your lover/husband/boyfriend/partner for constant moral support and comfort—he is simply not equipped to be attuned to the nuances of female sensitivity and emotions. But more importantly, all this outpouring of emotion and drama is not healthy for a relationship. Dumping all the upsetting details of our lives does nothing to build a sexy, vibrant, strong relationship. Rather, it diminishes it and wears away at the power of the union.

Every marriage, every partnership, is its own Secret Garden. French women know this innately. And they care for this garden, this marriage, as tenderly and carefully as they might a real garden. They know that certain flowers will bloom during certain times of the year. They know that one needs to care for the garden, but not overdo this care, and not overweed, overplant. The French woman knows that there's a necessary balance between too much water and too little water. The Secret Garden of a marriage can be a magical place where a man and a woman discuss shared experiences, laugh together, make love, indulge in their own kinky vices, and yes, even occasionally gossip. Still, it's necessary to make sure that this garden does not get overrun with insignificant, unnecessary, complaint-filled conversations—"weeds," if you will. A French woman keeps out boring information such as how her hairdresser cancelled an appointment, or how she's gained five pounds and needs to give up desserts, or how she really thinks her best friend's new coat is the wrong color. The French woman protects *le Jardin Secret* she shares with her husband, making sure that it is a place of calm and sensuality that the two of them can retreat to and create a spectacularly sensual world that is just for them.

French Lessons

Turn down one invitation this week, but do it sweetly, mysteriously. Don't do it because I said so. Do it when you really don't feel like going out. Create your own Secret Garden. Think of what you have that builds your sense of pleasure, calm, and self-esteem. Join a club, secretly. Or begin a new hobby that no one knows about but you. Read a book, alone, and keep it private. Find a new café that is your secret place. Go to a matinee, but tell no one.

Practice the art of discretion. Do not tell your lover or potential lover or even your husband of all your adventures. Be wild in the bedroom, and yes, a lady out of the bed.

CHAPTER ELEVEN

How French Women Earn Their Reputation for Being So Sexy

FRENCH WOMEN can be frustratingly fascinating. Ask any American woman who's lost her man to a French woman. They seem impossible to compete with. They're so darn sexy and then they've got that accent. On top of that, they've got that *je ne sais quoi* (indefinable) attitude. How do they do it? How do they always seem to maintain that sense of spiritual freedom?

As American women, we like to believe in this idea that once we find a perfect boyfriend, or once we get married, we'll be finished. We'll be set for life. Our husband will be our constant companion, we'll feel safe, we'll have a best friend, a museum partner, someone who'll help us do our taxes, go on vacations with us, have children with us, and share our every disappointment and triumph. We dream of a man we will walk into the sunset with, happily knowing that we will never have to date again.

Why do we look forward to the time when we won't have to date? Because dating is not fun. Not American style, anyway. It's exhausting, time consuming, and expensive for the man and for us too, if you consider the cost of clothing, makeup, manicures, and waxing. There's a great deal of pressure, because with the traditional American date, we are taken off the "market" and confined to one man who is on a mission to bed us and we must make a decision fast—do we want him to become our "boyfriend" or not? Do we want to sleep with him or not? Every date brings the "relationship" to a new and heightened level of intimacy. By the third date, we are often expected to consummate things. But, wouldn't it be nice to have more time? To wait and consider many options, many men, before having to choose one? Waiting, circulating, being seen, and being free are always to a woman's advantage.

Here's what one French woman told us:

> Go on with your life. Don't wait for his calls. When he calls the next time, you are busy whenever he asks you to do something . . . but you can suggest an alternate day (e.g., him: "What are you doing tomorrow night?"; you: "Oh, I have plans this week, but I'm free Sunday afternoon"). That way, you skirt the nights, even if you want him (this is, of course,

only if you want more than just sex) . . . If he
calls you to go out that night, don't. That means
he just wants to sleep with you.

This might sound very pragmatic and even a little cynical to an American woman who dreams of meeting "the
one" and finally getting married. The idea that we have to
go through this process of ignoring a man who doesn't
call makes us feel as if we're wasting time. We were brought
up to be proactive. To ask for what we want. And so we
think we should be able to just call the guy and say, why
aren't you asking me out for another date? But we all know
this doesn't work. Not in the long run, anyway.

Stop Dating

If we have not built a coterie of friends and we have found
our mate through the exhausting and tedious one-on-one
system of dating, by the time we get to the point where
we have a boyfriend, we just want to collapse. We want
to close the door and lock it. Get into bed, hold onto that
man, and never let him go. We're exhausted. We do not
want to flirt with anyone else, we've had it with men and
their "wicked" ways, we just don't ever want to go out on
a date with another man ever again. We found our prince
and that's that!

Unfortunately, this is not good for our relationship with
our boyfriend/husband/partner. This is because the very
notion of locking the door and collapsing into the relationship will soon lead to a sense of dissatisfaction. When

a couple does everything together and does not bring anything fresh to the relationship—and eliminates all the flirtations and friendships from their lives—they will find that boredom ensues. Just imagine it for a moment. It's like one of those thrillingly romantic vacations where you go to an island, just the two of you, and you have mind-blowing amazing sex—two or three or even four times a day. You walk hand in hand on the beach, you eat fabulous food, you drink delicious mojitos by the poolside, you stare into one another's eyes, hungrily. You have more sex and more food and more mojitos and by the fifth day of this, you want to get back to your real life. You need a change. Even Paradise can become tedious.

If you are in a marriage where everything is in place, the daily routine is set, and you go about your lives with order and discipline, there will come a time when you are bored. You long for the holiday in St. Martin's. And if this is not forthcoming, then you or your mate may become restless and seek out fantasy and escape outside of the relationship.

French women know that in order to keep their man intrigued and to keep their relationship exciting, alive, and growing, they need to mix things up and yes, change.

Les Petites Jalousies

Recently, during my travels to France, I observed a most delightful example of how the French use little jealousies to spice up their love affairs. I was at a dinner party. There were four of us—our lovely French hostess and my friend, a very pretty American woman. There was also a handsome French man, and me *une femme d'un certain âge*, who was there simply researching a book, and not interested in starting up *une liaison*.

We were enjoying a delicious dinner, with lots of wine, and laughing and chatting. The young American woman and I had just returned from Burgundy and she began telling a funny story about an incident we had along the way. Now, I knew she was extra animated in order to impress the French man. They had had an affair some years back and so there were sparks flying. And too, she wanted to make him a little bit jealous. And so she told the story of how she and I had been entertained by some men in a bar in Auxerre, and that one of the men, who worked for a tourism agency, gave us gifts before we left—maps, brochures, a book on the local history. My friend continued to describe how the gentleman wanted her to stay in town, and how he was *très séduisant* (very seductive).

She addressed all of us, but really the story was for the benefit of the French man. To make him a little bit jealous. However, interestingly enough, in the middle of this lively and very amusing story, the young French man turned to me and began solely addressing me, his eyes dancing, his teeth so white. And suddenly it seemed as if I was the most fascinating woman in the world to him! Now, I was pleased by the lovely attention, but I also knew that this was not for my benefit. I am, after all, old enough to be his mother. No, he was playing his own little game.

Everyone Benefits from Flirtation

He didn't suddenly realize he wasn't in love with my friend, and rather in love with me. He sensed that she was trying to make him a little jealous by showing him that there were other men in the world who found her very attractive, and to let him know that she has many other opportunities to find love. And it worked, he was a little jealous and so he decided to show her that he too was attractive and could find other opportunities. I could see through this and still, I felt lifted by his charms. And, I even found myself flirting back.

My American friend saw this going on in her peripheral vision and so she became even more dramatic, entertaining our hostess even more.

Nothing nefarious or manipulative was going on here. It simply shows how the art of conversation and little jealousies can enliven our relationships and make our lives just a little more fun. French women know that it is much more powerful to show a man that there are others out there who find them attractive than to complain, *"Why don't you pay more attention to me?"* This gets us nowhere, because in fact, if we are asking for more attention, we appear insecure and needy, and well, this is truly not attractive. French women know that men love a challenge—the challenge of the unknown and the unconquered. By remaining mysterious, flirting lightly and in the presence of your man, you show that you are still not completely conquered and that there are others who will always be waiting in the wings. The French woman knows that the secret to keeping her relationship alive and well is through the possibility of change, and the impermanent nature of life.

Nobody Owns Anybody Else

French women understand that men will begin to lose focus once they perceive they *possess* a woman, so a French woman will remain mysterious, even to her husband. This might mean changing a routine, doing something surprising, suddenly going away for a weekend with a friend. It might mean wearing something unusual, cooking a new dish, changing her hairstyle. This subtle action is enough to alert her man that he has not quite figured her out, that she is still a mystery.

Men Love a Happy Woman

The French woman's Secret Garden certainly helps her to reconnect with her source of strength, replenish her energies, and get in touch with her psyche. When she returns to "the real world" she brings a little mystery with her. And she's happier. Her man can sense something new—the "air" of having been someplace different, even secretive, and he begins to pay more attention to her. He pays more attention, not because she has asked him to, but because through her gestures, she has *shown* him that she is not completely dependent upon him for her joy, that she has hidden resources, and that unless he is careful, he could lose her.

French Women Are Theatrical

French women are a little theatrical when it comes to the first time they sleep with a man. While the man might think she suddenly "surrendered" to his seductions, she often actually plans the grand event weeks (maybe even months or years) in advance. She does so, first of all, by always being ready for intimacy—always wearing beautiful lingerie, always bathing with perfumed soaps, always taking care of her skin with creams and lotions, and always keeping at least one bottle of good champagne in her fridge. This way, she feels beautiful and confident and so she can truly allow herself to be carried away by the sexuality, the physicality, and the passion of the first time. She is not worried about the state of her apartment or embarrassed about dry skin. She is certainly not worried about her underwear!

Think of it as a little like feng shui, the ancient Chinese art of arrangement of objects in space that allow for the right flow of chi (or good energy). If you create a psychic "path" in your life (by wearing lingerie, keeping your home welcoming, being strong and independent) you leave room for love to find its way to your front door. There is no tension, no sense of neediness, no sense of blocked energy. You feel good and strong about yourself and so a man feels good about entering into your space.

Love Is in the Air

And the French man is also prepared for the event, because a French woman will not invite a man into her home alone unless she wants to sleep with him. He will have seen her home with a group of friends, perhaps at a dinner party, but once he's invited alone, he knows that she is prepared to be intimate. This way, there are no missed signals. Both the man and the woman know that the evening will end in the bedroom. This creates a wonderful sense of anticipation. All through dinner, the air of romance is heightened. The champagne is delicious. There are candles and music. She will make a fabulous meal and most likely serve chocolate mousse for dessert.

Still, even after the relationship is consummated, the French woman will not cut off contact with her friends and family. She will not end her relationships with members of her coterie and she will certainly not give up her Secret Garden. In fact, she knows that this support system will be even more necessary in keeping her man intrigued. She knows that once a man feels he has made her his conquest, the French woman must do whatever she can to reassert her mystery and independence.

French Women Take Their Time

French women don't believe in fast food and they don't believe in fast-food sex. True, there are instances when a French woman might indulge in an adventure or two, but only with the utmost discretion. In most matters of love, French women like to take their time, enjoying the pleasures of flirtation, seduction, and intrigue. Just as food is all about the sensual pleasures of eating—the different tastes and flavors, the conversation around the dinner table, the textures and spices—and oh, the wine—so too, the French woman enjoys love, romance, and flirtation as a sensual pleasure that takes time to truly appreciate. She knows that a little flirtation today may take months or even years to blossom. She's in no hurry, because she knows the value of time.

French Lessons

WHETHER THERE IS A MAN in your life or not, begin living your life as if passion is right around the corner. Clean your house, keep scented candles on hand, champagne in the fridge, and always wear beautiful lingerie. Oh, and shave your legs!

Next, change something about yourself. Buy a piece of jewelry and don't explain how and where you bought it. Go away for the weekend with a friend, but do not go into a lot of details as to why you're going.

Finally, if there is a man in your life who's been truly neglecting you and misbehaving, then cut him loose. Do it graciously and gracefully. If he's meant to be, he'll come back.

If you are happily married, plan a romantic surprise for you and your husband. Remember not to work too hard at it. Simply enjoy it.

CHAPTER TWELVE

⌒

Mariage à la Mode

French Women Accept Men for Who They Are

FRENCH WOMEN DON'T BELIEVE in the concept of Mr. Right. They don't believe in perfection. In fact, one French woman in Besançon explained the French philosophy when it comes to marrying a man this way: *"When you enter into a relationship, you accept who they are and don't try to change them."* She went on to tell us how in France, they don't make a big deal over anniversaries or special dates. Perhaps for a big anniversary—the tenth or the twenty-fifth—they might have a small family party.

And there's no fuss over Valentine's Day! There's no pressure on either men or women to *prove* how much they love the other. Love is more private, unspoken. It's not a competition with our best friends, to see whose husband or boyfriend is the bigger spender, the most romantic. French women are confident and they accept a man for who he is and not who society says he should be. She doesn't try to remake him.

The whole idea of the makeover is not very French. French women have a *laissez-faire* philosophy and believe in accepting each other's foibles, the good and the bad—especially after they are already in a relationship. French women believe in enjoying their lives and enjoying love. French women know that no one man is ever going to fulfill all their needs. They depend on family and friends. They are often very close to their mothers. They stay close to their childhood cohorts and *des amis de l'université* (their friends from college). Even when married, they keep up their coterie, because they know that this is as necessary to their well-being as fresh air and sunshine. They don't have the idea that they are "unfinished" until they find Mr. Right, get married, have children and then are "done."

This very idea of *being done* is not French.

After years of togetherness, French men and women do not start wearing matching baseball caps or *anything* that matches, for that matter. The French woman knows that her differentness, her femaleness, is what caught her husband's eye in the first place. It's the thing that challenges him. Think about it. If we allow ourselves to become a twin companion to our lovers and husbands, always agreeing with them, wearing similar clothes, agreeing with everything they say, well, then, all the spice will soon be gone. This is when a man strays. He needs a challenge. So, never give up. Always maintain your individuality and your separateness.

Vive la Différence

This is what a French woman will do. She will continue to grow and change and evolve her entire life. She finds new passions. She does this for herself, not for her man. And while she is pursuing her passions and tending to her Secret Garden, she is also out in the world, meeting other people. Meeting other men. And so, she continues to build her coterie. She has male friends as well as female friends. And of course, married French women give lots of dinner parties, where both couples and singles might mingle. All this puts her husband/partner on notice: she is a force in the world, she is admired, and if he starts to drift or neglects her, there will be other men to take his place.

One of the main reasons a married French woman will not collapse into the relationship is that she knows there are a lot of other women out there, beautiful women, flirtatious women, who would willingly take her place. One French woman told us how surprised she was by her Irish friend who talked of her marriage as "forever," assuming that once her vows were said, everything was carved in stone and she didn't really feel the need to make a great effort anymore to be seductive or feminine. Our French friend went on to tell us *"You always need to treat a relationship like it is new, and can end."*

And a French man told us this: *"Le mystère de la femme française c'est que son homme sait qu'il peut la perdre à tout moment."* (The mystery of the French woman is that her man knows he can lose her at any moment.)

At Any Moment

And yes, it's true, there is a downside to all this. And some French people do have lovers and mistresses. It would seem that simply knowing this keeps the passion alive and the spouse or partner alert. No one in France sinks into complacency in their partnership. The French know that there is always someone who could steal their lover away from them. This is a reality and so it makes them always try a little harder and look and act their best. They are always on the lookout for other admirers. And yes, yes, yes, even an occasional lover or mistress—although this is not as accepted as Americans seem to think.

The Myth of the Mistress

Ever since French President François Mitterand's mistress showed up at his funeral and stood side by side with Mitterand's wife, Americans have been buzzing. They've compared this with President Bill Clinton's problems and so the dialogue goes something like this—*"Oh, those French! They are so progressive! Look at that! They don't mind when their men keep both a mistress and a wife. Everyone is cool with that."* The assumption is (and our American men love to promote this notion) that most French men keep a mistress, in addition to their wives, and French women are absolutely fine with that. Our American men seem to forget about the myth of French women all having lovers. Mostly, they like to fantasize about the open-mindedness of French women. Perhaps this is partly why we all have a major crush on the French.

Here's what Maurice, a middle-aged French man, told us:

> Americans look for an ideal candidate, with a beautiful
> family, someone that they would like to be or
> someone who seems like a nice guy. Sorry if I
> simplify. The French have very little expectations
> from their politicians. A politician is viewed as a
> shark, a crook, and you can never trust one. You
> don't want to be their friend and you just know
> that you have to put up with them. You usually try
> to find the person that seems to be the least worst
> guy out of the bunch. Which is pretty hard!
>
> So, if Mitterand had a wife and a famous
> mistress, and a famous kid out of wedlock, it's true
> that we don't think that he should resign because
> of it, but it's also true that this is not the example
> that we aspire to.
>
> We didn't think that Clinton had to resign
> because he was caught with his pants down, it's
> going to be a big embarrassment for him, for sure,
> but it's not the end of the world and it's not like
> creating a whole plan to go into a fake war, if you
> see what I mean.

After conversations with many French women *and men*,
the truth is, French women do not generally tolerate their
husbands keeping a mistress. Of course, having affairs is
something that happens all over the world. Men have affairs and women have affairs. But it is not true that French
women don't get angry and jealous when they find out
their man is having an affair. They do. One French woman
told us this:

I don't believe it would still work out in our couple; it would be the end of it for us. I told my husband from the beginning: if you ever hesitate between me and another woman, I will make it very simple for you, there will be no more hesitating, you can go with the other and forget about me! Some might forgive . . . but it's just so hard to forget . . .

So, it sounds like this French woman is not so very different from American women. While the women we interviewed who were age forty and younger said they would never tolerate infidelity in a marriage or committed relationship, they did say that older women and women years ago did put up with their husbands' mistresses. However, those were economic arrangements. Women in the 1930s, 1940s, and 1950s did not have the financial wherewithal to leave a marriage once they discovered the mistress, and so they were forced to bite their tongues and put up with their husbands' infidelity. Contrary to myth, they were not fine with this, and they were not happy. While some took lovers, most did not, but rather threw their energies into their home lives and children.

The Five to Seven

This refers to the hours of indiscretion. True, some French do have affairs. They're kept a secret from their spouses and they have a great little expression for it. Five to seven is the time after work and before the family or business dinner. It is a time when yes, lovers do meet in apartments, hotel rooms, even in the office itself. One American woman who has been living in France for many years said that affairs do take place and that lots of people have lovers—both men and women. Still, it is not *openly* accepted and it seems as if anyone you talk to about it says that they know someone *else* who is having an affair. The person you speak to is not having an affair and his wife or her husband is certainly not having five to seven quickie sex in a hotel room. Here's what our American friend told us that she observed about affairs while living in Paris:

> Yes, I believe it is more accepted here or at least tolerated. Both sexes are doing it but not necessarily both parties in a couple. Open marriage—no. Need for passion and romance—yes. People get married relatively young here without having had lots of partners nor relationships so it is inevitable they cheat later on. Lots and lots of people have lovers.

So, to clarify—yes, the French are having affairs.

No, they are not openly accepted. Yes, they are kept a secret. (Not so different from here in America.) And if a spouse or partner finds out, it can mean the end of the marriage or relationship. Everyone seems to know someone who has a mistress or a lover, but no one seems to believe that her or his own partner is actually cheating on them. It's simply not out in the open. When we interviewed single French women, they did tell stories of how they'd been approached by married men to have affairs. Here's what one French woman in her early thirties told us:

On one side, you have the person who does not even think about cheating on the other one. And on the other side, the person who cheats on the other one.

Of course for the last scenario, when you happen to have a mistress or a lover, it is a secret, you don't of course tell it to your mate. You may confess it to your best friends, but this is it. The one who is cheated on is often the last one to know what is going on.

She went on to tell us how she has "happily" married male friends who go from mistress to mistress. Married ex-boyfriends have approached her to become their mistress. Some married men will only choose married women for an affair and meet at work or see each other in hotels at lunchtime. Some French men meet their mistresses on the Internet, and begin liaisons because they are bored with their marriages and an affair offers new and exciting possibilities. These men do not want to leave their wives and children, but they are looking for some adventure. Their wives know nothing of this and if they did, French women assure me, *"There'd be a big mess."*

But this too is true for married (or involved) French women. They are often tempted by another man and may have an affair. Sometimes they do not. In any event, it actually doesn't sound so much different from infidelity in America. We all know it goes on, perhaps not to the extent it does in France, but in both countries it is not generally openly accepted.

Be the Mistress in Your Marriage

The key is to never allow the home to become so familiar that we no longer "see" one another. And as women, we need to strive to make our lovers and our husbands notice us and not take us for granted. The first step to being the mistress in your own marriage is to get out of the house. I have a good American friend who has created what she calls "The Hotel Cure." This is a simple and very practical solution to the marriage bed doldrums. Every six weeks or so, she arranges to meet her husband in a hotel room. Sometimes it's just one night and sometimes it's for a weekend, but it always enlivens their relationship.

A little separateness can also create yearning and desire. The key is to find what makes you interesting and embrace it. Find the thing that originally attracted your mate to you and rediscover who you are outside of the union. Do things that make you happy.

Men know that a woman who is happy, who feels confident and sexy and really good about herself, is a willing and ready lover. She is not distracted by thoughts of how her buttocks have dimples or how she should really do something about her messy office or how she really, really needs to lose ten pounds. A confident, sexy, happy woman is free to romp and have some fun. She is free to be sexual and her mind is free to enjoy the pleasures of intimacy.

When we leave our insecurities at the door, we are free to give and receive pleasure. French women love to please their men. This isn't about sacrificing what they want. There is a certain philosophy among the French that the true joy of lovemaking comes not from one's own pleasure, but first from pleasing their partner. And this isn't a sexist comment, because when you talk to both French men and French women, they will say it is all about pleasing their intimate partner.

Men all over the world want to please us, and so how can we help them in this quest? So often when we get married, we stop trying to please. For many of us, during courtship, we are goal driven—we want to seduce and impress our lovers so that they will eventually want us for keeps, for all time, forever and ever. We might try to hide our shortcomings or emphasize our assets. We lose weight, buy new clothes, and take up a hobby that we believe will impress the object of our affection. And then once we are married, we "relax." We forget about the diet. We wear the same old clothes. We forget all about the hobby. We worry about the day-to-day chores. We may even begin to look on our mate as an extension of ourselves. And as we become more and more familiar with our partner, we become less and less exotic, fascinating, foreign, confusing, and challenging. On one level, this is lovely, this familiarity, but truthfully it is the death of romance and intrigue. The worst part of this is that we stop going out and tending to our coterie. And because our husband or partner doesn't see other men flirting with us, he can grow complacent and he can forget that *"the mystery of a woman is that a man knows that at any moment, he can lose her."*

This is why the married French woman will be sure to spend some time apart from her husband. She will go and visit friends in another part of the country for a few days and return with a fresh outlook.

One French woman told us that she keeps her marriage lively by being imaginative in bed. She said, *"You have to not be shy in bed! If he has some fantasies, it's good to play along!"* So, yes, you can be the mistress in the marriage. It's about having fun and a sense of theatre and being more than a little bit French.

And now you can be all those things. All you need is a little perfume, some good lingerie, a few recipes, a coterie of friends, a pair of sexy shoes, and a lot of attitude!

Et voilà, you are now a French woman!

French Lessons

SURPRISE YOUR HUSBAND/PARTNER with a new look. Don't say anything about it, just subtly change something about yourself. Invite friends to a dinner party at your home and if you've let your coterie disappear, work on rebuilding it. Get into a lively conversation with a handsome man and make sure your husband sees this, so that he is reminded (subtly) that he could lose you if he's not careful.

If you feel things have become dull, try "The Hotel Cure." Be sure to bring champagne and plenty of delicious lingerie along.

◝⁓⁓

CHAPTER THIRTEEN

How to Be a French Woman While Living in America

YOU MAY NOT HAVE ONE DROP of French blood in your body, but you can still be a "French Woman." The truth is, we are all a little French when it comes to love and romance. That's because the French culture is a culture of femininity and beauty, so it rightfully belongs to all the women of the world and it's ours to claim as our own. Even if you've never traveled to France and you don't know one single French person, you can get in touch with your true cultural roots as a woman. Start by reading Helena Frith-Powell's *All You Need to Be Impossibly French*. Debra Ollivier's *Entre Nous: A Woman's Guide to Finding Her Inner French Girl*. Rent some classic French films—*Belle de Jour, A Man and a Woman, Amélie, Girl on a Bridge*. Study Catherine Deneuve. Read *Madame Bovary* and *Le Divorce*.

Read everything by Véronique Vienne! Buy a beautiful scarf and experiment with wearing it in a variety of different ways. Attend a lecture at your local Alliance Française or take a class in conversational French for travelers. Join a wine-tasting group that specializes in French wines. Read *French Women Don't Get Fat* and begin eating like a French woman. And here's a little study guide to get you started.

1. *Stop Dating*. French women don't date. They have a coterie of men. Start by getting off the dating tread-mill and meet your man in the context of a group of friends and admiring men. Throw a dinner party, go out after work with your coworkers, invite him to meet you for a walk—anything that shows you off in the context of lots of men, and gets you out of the 2-hour interview-style date.

2. *Throw a Party*. Invite old and new friends. It's *très* French to mix up the sitting arrangements so it's male/female. Don't tell any one man you've got de-signs on him. Keep him guessing. Show off your culi-nary and entertaining skills.

3. *Walk the Walk*. French women walk everywhere. Yes, it's great exercise, but they do it to be seen. When you go for a walk with a potential lover, he doesn't know it's a date. He's not paying for anything, so there's no quid pro quo. Best of all, with a walk, he sees other men looking at you, so he knows there's competition.

4. *Get Offline and Get in Line*. French women meet men in the real world at museums, films, bars and parties. Being charming and a little seductive is a matter of

survival, so they'll chat up everyone. That's how they meet so many men.

5. *Fraternize on the Job.* Ditch the genderless business suit and wear something a little bit come-hither. French women aren't shy when it comes to meeting men at work.

6. *Be Natural.* The French look is a natural look. This means choosing one body part to show off, say a short skirt paired with a buttoned-up sweater. Or red lipstick with completely un-made-up eyes and no blush. Oh, and throw away the blow-dryer. French women don't fuss with their hair, but rather go for the tousled, wind-blown look.

7. *Say Hello to Your Ex.* French women leave old boyfriends on good terms. You never know when you'll need a date or someone to add to your coterie.

8. *Create a Coterie.* This is the all-important group of friends made up of men, women, coworkers, and new crushes. French women will go out in groups to movies and bars, museums and concerts. Again, it's another opportunity to see and be seen.

9. *Get Smart.* Even if you're not really smart, carry a book and wear those spectacles. French women know that being brainy is hot.

10. *Don't Pack Away the Good China.* What are you saving it for? French women use the good stuff for everyday. It's one of the secrets to their incredible confidence.

11. *Lingerie!* And they don't pack the lace panties away either. French women wear sexy lingerie every day. Oh, and the bra and panties must always match. Another thing that makes them so confident.

12. *Get Cooking.* Yes, French women have known it for centuries and we just didn't quite believe it, but it's true: the way to a man's heart is through his stomach.

13. *Love the Skin You're In.* The secret to self-love is fragrant creams and lotions. The French love perfume and anything that gives them an opportunity to feel good in their own skin. This is the secret to their confident walk—that and the fact that their mothers told them to *hold their heads up high and stand up straight!*

14. *Tend to Your Secret Garden.* Le Jardin Secret. This is a euphemism for a place or even a person the French woman goes to when she wants to shore up her inner resources. You can be more French by keeping a secret—whether it's your obsession with nineteenth century medical journals or the crush you've got on the guy at Starbucks. It's so American to be honest and tell everything. Try keeping some secrets.

15. *Less Is More.* Try buying just one great skirt this season. Eat smaller portions. French women don't believe in supersizing anything. They make do—not just with food and clothes, but with their man. They don't try to change him, but accept him for who he is.

16. *Stand by Your Man*. See above.

17. *Vive la Différence*. French women are women and they won't let you forget it. Wear something feminine to work. Try traveling in a skirt with boots—you'll find you get a lot more attention—and help with your luggage!

18. *You Have a Right to Be Moody*. You are *ze woman*. He is *ze man*. You are passionate! You have *ze problem* with that?! Reclaim your right to be a woman, to be moody and capricious and emotional. Life is a whole lot more fun when you're not trying to act sane all the time!

Acknowledgments

I AM VERY GRATEFUL to so many people who helped me with this delicious project, but without my friend, my translator and the most fun traveling companion a gal could ask for—Jessica Lee—this book would not be possible. Big thanks to my wonderful agent, Irene Goodman and my editor extraordinaire, Audrey LaFehr. And I am especially thankful to Isaure Mignotte, who worked tirelessly to check the French translations and to make sure I got the accent marks in the right places!

In writing this book, there were so many French women and men and American Francophiles who opened their doors and hearts to me, who shared their recipes and their secrets and passionate opinions—well, it's hard to begin. Nonetheless, I want to especially thank Nancy Flavin, Sylvie Gourlet, Marie-Joëlle Jobevalot and Marjorie Van Halteren for hosting us and showing us how the French truly live.

I thank Carol Merriman for her encouragement and for coming up with my title! I thank Robin Lillianthal for all things philosophical, Devin Norwood, my personal guru, Werner Sieber, for his enduring friendship, Paula Martin, who believed in me when I didn't believe in myself, Beverly Aker, for her fabulous copyedits, and Laurie Graff and Deborah Kainin, for always inspiring me.

I wrote much of this book at the Virginia Center for the

Creative Arts, and I thank them for their generous writing fellowship.

Last, but not least, I thank my father, my daughter, and my husband who has always supported my desire to truly express my inner French girl!